ISRAEL II

BEYOND THE

BASICS

K. J. FROLANDER

www.IsraelBasics.com

ACKNOWLEDGEMENTS

Thanks to my Inverness Vineyard Church Israel small group students who helped refine me this final project by asking the most terrific questions.

Special thanks to all my beta readers. Robyn Korn, Courtney Hudson, Joan Walker, Becki Brechin, Sue Fattibene, Crystal Cook, Marguerite Amaya, Michael Cory, Jerry Frolander, J Downes and Pastor Bubba Justice. I appreciate all your time, input, advice and encouraging comments more than I can say.

Thank you again to Diane Withers who first introduced me to the Jewish roots in Christianity in 2006 through her riveting small group teachings and most amazing field trip ever!

Thank you to Yeshua most of all for the time and grace, attention, connections and revelations. You afforded me while encouraging me to "write it all down." You are the best!

TABLE OF CONTENTS

INTRODUCTION: WHY SHOULD CHRISTIANS STUDY ISRAEL?

There is coming a day when each of us will have to decide whether or not to support and bless Israel. This day is probably coming very soon based on the way world politics are aligning. The middle ground of ignorance that many now enjoy will collapse. Jerusalem is designed by God as a cup of poison, drunkenness or reeling for the nations (Zechariah 12:2). Already, Israel is more divisive than other political issues, and in the end, Israel will be the *only* issue. World circumstances will be in upheaval and tumult.

Not only will God allow some pretty dramatic and horrible things to happen, His justice is behind them happening. It is at His command that his angels will be pouring out the bowls of wrath where 1/3 of the population will die, 1/3 of the fish and animals too. At today's population level that is over 2.3 billion people...BILLION! And we in the U.S. have demanded to know where God was when 4 people died at the hand of terrorists in Boston.

People, and probably you too, will be asking, "How could a loving God allow these things to happen?" or "Why would God let so many children die?" or dogs, or my garden or livelihood?" If you as a Christian don't know the answers, who can unbelievers turn to? The question of whether God is trustworthy and faithful to His Word must be settled in your heart already, before you are put to the test, or you will not be able to trust

God's goodness when it doesn't look like you expect "good" to look. Your heart might become offended with God because He has not done what you thought He should in your life, or someone else's life.

If a man's heart becomes offended, he is likely to turn away from God in the most adverse circumstances he will ever experience. There will be no comfort; and how hopeless life will be for him.

Satan is planning to set up world circumstances to appear that peace would come to earth just by getting rid of tiny little Israel. It will be said that Israel is the thorn in the world's side, that one small group of people's presence in a particular location should not be allowed to dictate what happens in the entire world. But that will be the hook, the trap, that will ensnare people. Israel is the final line drawn in the sand. And actually God is behind it all, because He is after our hearts. He wants hearts that beat for the things that He loves.

The State of Israel will do things in the natural that we won't agree with…they're only human after all. But Christians were designed by God as the grafted-in branch of the Olive Tree (Israel) in order to support Israel in her calling (Romans 11).

When Israel does things we don't agree with, we have to have already made our decision to support her anyway.

God's promise in Genesis 12:3 still stands true, and was given without condition. "Those who bless you I will bless, those who curse you I will curse." God is referring to Israel in this statement.

Also scripture says that in the end all the nations will gather against Israel (at the Valley of Armageddon). All means all. The U.S. who has been Israel closest modern friend will at some future date betray that friendship and Israel will stand alone. Alone except for the God she is in covenant relationship with! But just because your nation (where ever you are from) does not bless Israel, doesn't mean *you* can't! Individuals and hopefully all Christians will stand in support of Israel at that last great Battle!

If we have not made the decision to stand with Israel no matter what while we have the time to study under easy life circumstances, while Israel is our ally, then we will not be able to understand what God is doing in the last days when it is imperative to stand with Israel. At that time, life and standing with Israel will both be hard!

Supporting the Apple of God's eye will set people free to be blessed by God; but turning our backs to God's Chosen People is choosing to set ourselves against God, choosing to be cursed.

You do not want to have to make this choice under the duress of the coming times. Decide now. This second book in the Israel Basics Series, goes beyond *Israel Basics: What Every Christian Should Know* to give you more details and a more in depth view of what God is doing in the earth, with His chosen people, with you, and more.

People who don't understand Israel and how she fits into God's unfolding plan don't fully understand their Bible. It is a strong statement, I know. Think of it like this, God's unfolding plan or adventure romance story is like the *Lord of the Rings* trilogy by JRR Tolkien. We are living out the tail end of the second book here in the 21st century. We are very familiar with our story (Christianity). We understand the symbolism, the language, how events are linked together for our part of God's story, not only because we are part of it, but because we study it on Sundays and we read our Bibles with our story in mind. Somewhere inside us, perhaps even buried in our consciousness, is the knowledge that our story will be continued in another book (Tolkien's third book or the Millennial Kingdom). However not many have looked at the full picture by digging into the first book (Israel's story). There are entire segments, symbolism and languages of communication with our Author's story that we are missing because we assumed the story started with us. By dismissing the first part of the story we have diminished our own and what the Author was presenting.

When you understand what God is doing and saying through Israel you bring fullness to your own identity. You can better understand your God-designed roll in this "story #2" of Christianity and your coming roll in the finale story where God wraps everything up. The guy (Yeshua) gets the girl (the Church & Israel as one new man, the Bride of Christ), the evil empire (hell) is conquered forever and the bad guys (Satan & demons) will be thrown in the Lake of Fire forever. This is true justice!

It is the best story in the world; it is the *only* story in the world. Every scene we live plays into the final outcome. Every word is influential, every action significant. We work and worship every minute, for our great King or against Him.

Psalm 107:43 (NLT)
Those who are wise will take all this to heart;
they will see in our history the faithful love of the Lord.

1

WORLDVIEW

HISTORICAL WORLDVIEW

We live inside a sweeping love story. Our story began at the Beginning and has more twists and turns than all the soap operas ever written. It is God's story, and only He can recite all of history.

Since we are only human, we break history into linkable parts in order to comprehend events of the past. Everyone uses a unique filter formed by our upbringing, our studies, our culture, and sometimes, a decision to adopt a new worldview. A person's worldview is how they understand history and the world and how they interpret historical and current events.

Their worldview or "grid" helps individuals organize and process mankind's progress over time in an understandable way. It is how we define progress that forms the differences in people's worldviews.

People use all kinds of filters to break history into their own grid. Communism, Secularism, Humanism, Buddhism, Christianity, Islamicism and hundreds more, and each produces a unique emphasis on historical events. People's differing ideologies come out of their differing worldviews; fundamentally different definitions of progress produce different ideas of where the future is headed and thus different goals.

Currently there are two deadly worldviews that are in competition for people: Radical Islamicism and Progressivism. Surprised that I would equate them? One wants to blow up freedom-loving people. The other wants to lull-to-sleep freedom-loving people all over the globe. They are both after power to rule the earth according to their worldview. But underneath, both are lies of Satan who has a goal to gain control. Since most people are familiar with Radical Islam's agenda, we will delve into what Progressivism's dangerous agenda looks like these days.

PROGRESSIVISM

"Progressivism" or the "progressive agenda" is something we in America have been hearing a lot about recently. It's also been called liberalism. (I'm not talking Republican versus Democrat here. Progressivism runs much deeper than an American political label.) The ideology of progressivism is a worldwide agenda that seeks to promote the past as dusty, old, worthless thinking that should be put away so that society and mankind can move on to a new, scientific way of thinking. Progressives want to evolve past anything old, traditional, established or time-honored. They have fabricated an entire past showing evolution as the natural progression of mankind in order to relieve modern society of a past created by a living God to Whom they are accountable.

They label themselves progressive, but what are they "progressing" toward? Many Progressives themselves don't know what they are striving for. Progressive ideals value equality among races, genders, and religious beliefs (except Christianity, because that represents the old, dusty way of thinking). They hate intolerance and injustice. They value choice and politically correct words so as not to offend anyone. They want to save nature, the environment and animals (all nature except unborn human babies). They want nature to remain natural, almost Eden like, even to the detriment of people and society. Progressives desire world peace. Progressives strive toward a central patriarchal figure with authority to rule everyone and enforce their worldview; they want a single seat of power in a government of peace.

Those are all God-breathed ideas that have been in place since the beginning of our love story. They are ways God created us to function. Unknowingly, in their hearts, Progressives are actually

> ### DON'T BECOME OFFENDED
> If you consider yourself progressive, please don't be offended. It is not your ideals that are under attack in this chapter. The *ideals* are great. The point is that apart from God, these great ideals cannot and will not succeed. The Progressive Movement in the earth is designed to do just that: to accomplish God's perfection in the earth *without* submitting to Him. The truth has been twisted by the enemy, and he has tipped his hand when we see all the exceptions to the rules inherent in the progressive worldview.

yearning for the Kingdom of God to come! A phrase in Isaiah 65:25 says, "The wolf and the lamb shall feed together," and foretells God's future peace and harmony. God implanted this utopia idea into the heart of man when He placed Adam in the Garden of Eden and walked with him there. When God made mankind, He formed our standard baseline as a picture of the coming Kingdom, where it will be a utopian community of peace. God modeled for mankind how to desire free-will and choice when He made man and gave him a choice to follow God or not. Justice and righteousness will be the basis of society in the earth (Psalm 89:14 & Isaiah 9:7). We are designed to worship, yet we jump off the right track if we worship anything created. We were made to worship the Creator and bring Him pleasure (Revelation 4:11). He is the single seat of power, the Father of all. The garden of our hearts will be in harmony with the God of the Universe. At that time, the world will be at peace too, because all hearts will be at peace in His right judgments.

This utopian kingdom is not a new idea, neither has God kept it secret. It has been revealed since the Beginning, and it is coming. Unfortunately, people who desire this kind of progress are out of order because it is chasing after the utopia in our own strength. When all is revealed, we don't want to be told what to do by a dusty set of rules which we can't measure up to and still "enjoy" life. We want the Eden, but without the Creator walking with us.

So Progressives who are promoting this worldview *do* want something that is righteous, good and functional. (We'll come back to this word, functional.) Unfortunately, they are going about it in a dysfunctional way. Progressive leaders are simply reenacting in our day the usurping of power that first happened in Heaven when Satan tried to take God's place. Satan entices men over and over again, whispering in their ears, "All this I will give to you, if you will bow down and worship me" (Matthew 4:9). Progressives are trying to create the coming Kingdom through their own power, with the goal of being the one in power when the kingdom is built. The position belongs to God alone!

NOT THE FIRST TIME AROUND THIS BLOCK

God set up the world, therefore He is in charge. Through mankind's (Adam and Eve's) sin, Satan gained dominion on the earth, and since then, he's been seeking more control and worship which rightfully belong to God. Jealousy has been his problem since he was an archangel in heaven. Satan's goal is to dethrone God so he can take full control of the Story, and he has used various groups—some more well-intentioned than others—through the millennia to gain control (i.e. many ancient civilizations, and "modernly" the Crusades, Spanish Inquisition, Darwinism, Muslim Sharia Law).

When we become believers and accept Jesus' payment for our sin, we set up a little piece of God's kingdom in this fallen world. Since we take away from Satan's control and power, he wants it back. Therefore, Satan has put into place long-standing, far-reaching plans to undermine what God is doing in the earth.

PROGRESSIVISM IS ADVANCED SECULARISM

The normal Western worldview today is called Secularism. Secularism sees the Bible through the grid that it is just a piece of ancient literature. People who hold a secular worldview look at the Bible critically. They categorize it with other pieces of ancient literature, proclaiming "there's nothing special about it." Secularists view the biblical period (Old Testament timeframe) when God's plan is unfolding in the earth through his people Israel, as "that's how life was then, but this is how it has evolved in modern times." That is old and dusty and needs to progress to a more scientific/modern idea and way of thinking. Secularism's emphasis is not on what God is doing, but the "evolution" of the people and civilization. That is why they highlight things throughout history and current society that agree with their particular worldview (i.e. get prayer out of schools, set up a media of politically-correct language police, provide "choice" for women with abortion on demand, etc.)

WHERE THE PROGRESSIVE WORLDVIEW IS LOGICALLY HEADED AND WHY

Both the Progressive Movement and God are moving the earth toward a one-world government. Again, this is not new. It has always been God's ultimate plan, and Satan has been trying to counterfeit it and make himself the ultimate ruler. The last time a person took this idea, ran with it, and almost brought it about was Hitler's Third Reich. But the first time it happened was in ancient Babylon with the Tower of Babel. Progressivism is humanism at its core. It comes out of some of the same philosophies as pagan Hellenism (more on that later).

Today, instead of just worshipping the sun, moon or stars as people did in ancient times, Progressives have taken the whole earth as their god. Now, the promoted worldview is all about balance, understanding a crime from a perpetrator's side with sympathy, being politically correct, bringing equality, no one being the winner or better than another, empowering the underdog...doesn't everybody root for the underdog? It makes you feel charitable and somehow a little better about yourself if the underdog "wins." Many times that underdog is not held to the same standard as the other side. The media tells stories in such a way that we are supposed to feel sorry for and coddle the "bad guy" because he's had too many obstacles to overcome from his childhood, instead of pointing out his need for a Savior and the forgiveness He offers. What is this mess? Why do we want to turn God's story upside down?

True equality looks like this: Everybody has sinned and needs the Savior. (Romans 3:23).

Unfortunately, progressive thinking is rampant in the Church too. Our churches take their cues from the media and secularized seminaries. We want a church that "makes me feel better in my everyday life," instead of one that uses scripture to correct us when we are off the path of righteousness. And there *are* areas where we are off. Have you ever mentioned praying for Israel or sending aid to Israel without some do-gooder who finds herself "informed and balanced" on the issues piping up, "but what about the poor Palestinians?"

This Progressive agenda in the promotion of their worldview goes back to the sinful root of pride in Babylon. And God tells us to come out of Babylon! (Revelation 18:4). The people of Babylon decided they needed to make a name for themselves (i.e. pride).

> **Genesis 11: 1-9** Now the whole world had one language and a common speech. As people moved eastward, they found a plain in Shinar (Babylonia) and settled there. They said to each other, "Come, let's make bricks and bake them thoroughly." They used brick instead of stone, and tar for mortar. Then they said, "Come, let us build ourselves a city, with a tower that reaches to the heavens, so that we may make a name for ourselves; otherwise we will be scattered over the face of the whole earth."
> But the LORD came down to see the city and the tower the people were building. The LORD said, "If as one people speaking the same language they have begun to do this, then nothing they plan to do will be impossible for them. Come, let us go down and confuse their language so they will not understand each other." So the LORD scattered them from there over all the earth, and they stopped building the city. That is why it was called Babel* (or Babylon[1])—

---

* The Hebrew word for Babel sounds like the Hebrew word which means "confused."[1]

because there the LORD confused the language of the whole world. From there the LORD scattered them over the face of the whole earth.

The whole tower rebellion took place in Babylon, but it didn't come out of a vacuum. What was going on in Babylon that led to the people of the world wanting to spit in God's face like this only about 200 years after flood?

BABYLON

Babylon is a strange mystery. It seems to be a prototype, the birthplace of group-effort rebellion (versus individual effort) to undermine what God had in His heart and His ultimate plan of redemption. In addition, at the end of days, Babylon is the location of the *final* rebellion as outlined in Revelation. The undisputed location is modern-day Iraq, near Baghdad.

> **Revelation 18:1-3** After this I saw another angel coming down from heaven. He had great authority, and the earth was illuminated by his splendor. [2] With a mighty voice he shouted: "'Fallen! Fallen is Babylon the Great!' She has become a dwelling for demons and a haunt for every impure spirit, a haunt for every unclean bird, a haunt for every unclean and detestable animal. [3] For all the nations have drunk the maddening wine of her adulteries. The kings of the earth committed adultery with her, and the merchants of the earth grew rich from her excessive luxuries."

> **Revelation 18:23-24** The light of a lamp will never shine in you again. The voice of bridegroom and bride will never be heard in you again. Your merchants were the world's important people. By your magic spell all the nations were led astray. In her was found the blood of the prophets and of God's holy people, of all who have been slaughtered on the earth."

In between these two civilizations, Babel and Baghdad, there are types of Babylons that crop up, recognizable by their civilization's intent on destruction of Israel: Egypt, Assyria, Babylon (again), Persia, Greece, the Seleucid dynasty, the Roman Empire, Mohammad's Muslims, the Church during the Crusade period, Spain, Hitler's Third Reich, and today, the Pan-Islamic state leadership in the Middle East and Europe.

HELLENISM AND GREEK THINKING

Hellenism is the pagan religion of Greece. Its popularity began around 323 BC and lasted well into the first century AD. Hellenism led to the influence of Greek thinking throughout the world. Greek thinking is the opposite of how God intended for us to think (Hebrew thinking). Alexander the Great in his mere 12 years of war campaigns managed to conquer quite a bit of the known world. His particular brand of conquering led to a complete change of a people's way of thinking, and the way and whom they worshiped.

The Hellenistic period occurred in the wake of conquests by Alexander the Great (356-323 BC), which extended across Anatolia, Syria, Phoenicia, Persia, Judea, Gaza, Egypt, Bactria, Mesopotamia, and as far east as Punjab in modern-day India. The period featured a fusion of Greek, Middle Eastern, and Indian culture. Under Greek dominance, Hellenistic subjects began to adopt elements of Greek fashion, urban life and religion. The etymology of "Hellenistic" comes from the word *Hellen*, which is the Greeks' name for themselves.[2]

The Greeks called themselves Helen. Therefore the religion of Hellenism at its base level is worship of self. You can see their self-worship in the prominence of nude sculpture in their society, and their promotion of pleasure, knowledge, and philosophy. Origins of Hellenism can be traced back to Homer, the blind poet who wrote *The*

Iliad and *The Odyssey* about the Trojan Wars and escaping society to rescue the beautiful Helen who had been lured away from her husband by the king of Troy. According to the *1906 Jewish Encyclopedia*, "The Hellenic influence pervaded everything, and even in the very strongholds of Judaism it modified the organization of the state, the laws, and public affairs, art, science, and industry, affecting even the ordinary things of life and the common associations of the people."[3]

Hellenism's influence was so deep that it changed the manner in which people think. The change in thinking patterns will be referred to from here forward as "Greek thinking." Greek thinking for the first time brought nebulous ideas into the world's collective conscious. Philosophers began to spout ideas. The Greeks became consumed with gaining knowledge, and they spread that insatiable quest wherever they went. The Greek was very concerned with the appearance of things. They introduced abstract images into the mind, such as purity, wickedness, righteousness. None of these words are concrete things; they are ideas of things. In a Hebraic context the ideas would be described differently, beyond just the difference in the sound of the language.

The Greeks did provide a dynamic and exact language with specific meanings and many, many words for our New Testament writing, but at what cost? We lost the concrete description words that could be sensed from touch, smell, taste, see, and hear in the original Covenant. We gained knowledge, but not action.

את

GREEK VERSUS HEBREW THINKING

Greek and Hebrew ways of processing information are totally different. They have opposite pathways and therefore opposite outcomes. William Barrett says,

> The distinction...arises from the difference between doing and knowing. The Hebrew is concerned with practice, the Greek with knowledge. Right conduct is the ultimate concern of the Hebrew, right thinking that of the Greek. Duty and strictness of conscience are the paramount things in life for the Hebrew; for the Greek, the spontaneous and luminous play of the intelligence. The Hebrew thus extols the moral virtues as the substance and meaning of life; the Greek subordinates them to the intellectual virtues...the contrast is between practice and theory, between the moral man and the theoretical or intellectual man. (As quoted in *Irrational Man* by Barrett.[4])

Where the Greek was concerned with appearance, the Hebrew was concerned with function. The Hebrew asks the question, "How is it supposed to work?"

Christianity seeks to understand the incomprehensible God in concrete, yet abstract, terms. But, "to the Jewish mind, the understanding of God is not achieved by referring (in) a Greek way to timeless qualities of Supreme Being, to ideas of goodness and perfection, but rather by sensing the living acts of His concern, to His dynamic attentiveness to man. We speak not of His goodness in general but of His compassion for the individual man in a particular situation."[6(p.21)] In other words, God is not "known" in the abstract, but in the specific situations into which He has asserted Himself. God is what He has revealed Himself to be, not what we have theorized Him to be.

Abram Heschel writes, "The Greeks learned in order to comprehend. The Hebrews learned in order to revere. The modern man learns in order to use."[6(p.34)] Modern people want a "technique-oriented" religion of utility. Wanting to apply the Bible to our lives is not wrong; it is the motivation of the modern heart that is off the mark. God gave us His Word to reveal Who He is, His heart toward us, and how He wants to relate to us. Generally, we set Him aside for our own goals of being able to "use" the information we are learning. The modern man wants techniques for understanding, systematizing and ordering our lives in seven easy steps. We want to learn the structure of the "prophetic timetable" so that we can know what's going to happen next or so that we can know when to stock food and flee into the mountains to await the Lord's return. Some people want to know the principles of the Bible so they can have something to market to other Christians.

"To try to distill the Bible, which is bursting with life, drama, and tension, to a series of principles would be like trying to reduce a living person to a diagram."[6(p.20)]

BENNER'S HEBREW VS. GREEK THINKING

"All five of the senses are used when speaking and hearing and writing and reading the Hebrew language. An example of this can be found in Psalms 1:3; "He is like a *tree* planted by *streams of water*, which yields its *fruit* in season, and whose *leaf* does not *wither*". In this passage we have concrete words expressing abstract thoughts, such as a tree (one who is upright, righteous), streams of water (grace), fruit (good character) and an unwithered leaf (prosperity)."[7]

Notice that Benner's addition of the words in parentheses are all Greek-thought based, to help us Western Greek thinkers understand. We have lost the concrete connections between things from which God intended for us to learn.

For example, a Greek concept of a pen is "something about 7-8 inches long, made from plastic, sometimes they have lids, and ink comes out one end." A Hebraic description of a pen is "something you write with." See the difference between Greek appearance and Hebrew function in the description?

Another example of a Greek concept: knee. The same concept in Hebrew thinking: the part of the body that bends.

Words in Hebrew are about identifying something by what it *does*, its action, not by its appearance. In a sense, even nouns in Hebrew are verbs. For example, "the Hebrew word for father is אב (av) and literally means 'the one who gives strength to the family' and mother אם (em) means 'the one that binds the family together'."[7]

Greek thinking imparts knowledge; Hebrew thinking imparts function. Therefore when God gave us His Word, it was not to impart knowledge, it was to impart function! God, our Creator, was telling us, "Here is how life is to function." If you remember, it was God who told Adam and Eve not to eat of the Tree of *Knowledge* of Good and Evil. Knowledge is only somewhat important. (I know your Greek mind just blew a gasket! You should probably read that sentence again.) What does knowledge accomplish anyway if not paired with function, with actually doing something? Nothing. It sits in your mind/heart and festers, it puffs up...oh wait! that's in the scripture:

23

I Corinthians 8:1b We know that "We all possess knowledge." But knowledge puffs up while love builds up.

HUMANISM

When Hellenism progressed to new generations, it was repackaged as humanism by the 1800's. It is alive and well in the USA and has invaded virtually every aspect of our lives with the permission from the U.S. Supreme Court who so ingeniously ruled that "Secular Humanism *is* a religion *"for free exercise clause purposes*," and it is *not* a religion *"for establishment clause purposes*."[8] Whether Humanism is recognized as a religion or not, it functions as one. It draws people away from the heart of God and propagates a worldview that sets itself up as a god.

To recap: Babylon, Hellenism, Humanism, Progressivism are all the same pagan worship, just re-branded to fit a "modern" society of people who think they know more than their ancestors. So much detail included here so you can see how Greek-thinking has influenced our daily life and even the process by which we think, even for born again believers!

את

OUR WORLDVIEW

Now to the good part. In this book, we will filter history through a biblical worldview which says that history can be understood through God's unfolding plan, or "God's Ultimate Plan."

THE BIBLICAL WORLDVIEW GRID:[9]

There is a God. He is pure. He made everything for His own purposes and enjoyment. He set up the rules of the universe that He made and then made mankind. Sin entered the world through man, yet God wanted a reconciled relationship with man, as He had in the beginning. So He chose a man (Abraham) from among men to be a light to the nations. God grew Abraham into a nation (Israel) to shine light into the world and be an example of how God loves and deals with mankind.

Because Israel was chosen to shine light into the world, Israel was given a code of conduct (Torah). The Torah set up the Hebrew people to be successful in all they do, *if* they follow the commands. They will be blessed with abundance; they won't get sick; they will multiply; they will be full of peace and joy (Deuteronomy 7:12-15). The Torah is not a rigid set of rules that are burdensome. It is the plan of God to prosper a people, to set them apart, to make them holy. The Torah was designed to elevate a people to live fully alive, connected to God, and as a representation of Him. The nations were to have seen a prospering nation of people (Jews) and been provoked to jealously ask, "What is it that makes life work for you?" and the Jew was to smile and say, "Come and meet my God!" thus, bringing the nations in repentance back to reconciliation in the heart of the Living God.[9]

> **Deuteronomy 4:6-8 NLT** Obey them (the laws and regulations) completely, and you will display your wisdom and intelligence among the surrounding nations. When they hear all these decrees, they will exclaim, 'How wise and prudent are the people of this great nation!' [7] For what great nation has a god as near to them as the LORD our God is near to us whenever we call on him? [8] And what great nation has decrees and regulations as righteous and fair as this body of instructions that I am giving you today?

The Jews were chosen to be a light to the world. Not that one nation was better than another, it was a choice. God's choice. God's ultimate plan continues to unfold daily in human choices and events.

Beyond just understanding the biblical worldview, we are going to go deeper. Because we are a western culture with its roots in Hellenism, most Christians in America study the Word of God though a Greek thought pattern to gain knowledge. However, in order to gain everything God has in store for us, we need to learn from a Hebraic perspective instead of a Greek one. "This will require a philosophical and intellectual paradigm shift on our part. It will mean coming (to) Scripture from an entirely different angle. It will mean learning to think like the Hebrew who thought more like God."[5]

This will provide some major shifting in what we thought we knew! And that is good.

END NOTES

1. Footnotes from Biblegatway.com "Genesis 11:9 That is, Babylon; *Babel* sounds like the Hebrew for *confused*." Retrieved December 6, 2012 from http://www.biblegateway.com/passage/?search=gen%2011& version=NIV#en-NIV-276

2. The Wise Geek website. 2003-2013. The Conjecture Corporation. Retrieved December 6, 2012 from http://www.wisegeek.com/what-should-i-know-about-the-hellenistic-period.htm

3. Hellenism. 1906. *The Jewish Encyclopedia.* Retrieved December 6, 2012 from http://www.jewishencyclopedia.com/articles/7535-hellenism

4. Barrett, William. 1962. *Irrational Man: A Study in Existential Philosophy.* Archor Books/Doubleday.

5. Knowles, Brian. (n.d.) The Hebrew Mind vs. the Western Mind. Retrieved Dec 7, 2012 from http://www.godward.org/Hebrew%20Roots/hebrew_mind_vs__the_western_mind.htm

6. Heschel, Abraham. 1976. *God in Search of Man.* Farrar, Straus, and Giroux Publishing p. 20.

2

HEBREW WORDS BRING UNDERSTANDING AND FUNCTION

As we just learned, Hebrew thinking is about function and Greek thinking is about knowledge or abstract learning. Our very way of thinking is of a Greek mindset instead of a Hebraic mindset. A Hebraic mind is what God designed from the beginning of time. Every time we change part of God's design, it loses some value He intended. The thought process differences can be boiled down to that Greek thinking is concerned with appearance; it explains things in abstract images in your mind, and Hebraic thinking describes things according to your five senses and is concerned with function. God is so much more practical than abstract thinking!

Remember the pen descriptions? In a Greek description, a pen is a slender object, long, some have caps, they contain ink that comes out one end. A Hebraic description of a pen is "something you write with." If it is not something you can see, smell, taste, hear or feel, it does not exist in the Hebrew world or even the language. That is one of the reasons that the Bible is so filled with agricultural comparisons, it is so down to earth, so practical. We have made the Scripture so weird and difficult at times because we filter a Hebraic text through a Greek mindset. When there is something we don't understand, it should be a flashing light to dig deeper and change the way we are looking at it. Instead, we usually put it on the back burner and let it simmer until it's gone. Let's change that and ask God to open our minds to what He is saying.

COINCIDENCE

The word *coincidence* does not exist in the Hebrew language. Everything always involves the Lord's long reaching plans and purposes. Sometimes He uses miracles to bring them about if necessary.

FUNCTION VS DYSFUNCTION

Naming or calling something from the Hebrew mindset tells us how something is to function, and we can see this in scripture from the very beginning:

> **Genesis 1:3-5** Then God said, "Let there be light"; and there was light. [4]And God saw the light, that *it was* good; and God divided the light from the darkness. [5]God called the light Day, and the darkness He called Night. So the evening and the morning were the first day.

God pronounces the light as good (Hebrew word: *tov*), but "good" is a concept word for which we in the west have lost the Hebraic root meaning. We usually compare good to bad or to evil. That sort of comparison is not meant in the Hebraic context of the word *tov*. When God is saying that something is good, He means it is functioning

30

within the design for which He made it. The same is true all the way through the creation story. God spoke something into being and then called it *"tov."* It is almost as if His calling it good caused it to work within its function.

WHAT IS MAN'S FUNCTION?

Genesis 1:26-27 gives us an inkling:

> Then God said, "Let us make mankind in our image, in our likeness, so that they may rule over the fish in the sea and the birds in the sky, over the livestock and all the wild animals, and over all the creatures that move along the ground." So God created mankind in his own image, in the image of God he created them; male and female he created them.

Genesis 2:7 fills in more detail: "Then the LORD God formed a man from the dust of the ground and breathed into his nostrils the breath of life, and the man became a living being."

So, man was formed out of the dust of the earth, made in God's likeness, filled with the breath of God's life, and given authority to rule over fish, birds, animals and creatures.

Let's examine the whole passage Hebraically by asking "What is man's function?" (We don't care what the garden or man look like because appearance is the Greek way of viewing things.) We are concerned now with function. If we don't understand how it works, its function, it is of no benefit to us. God is not just giving knowledge to fill our brains in Genesis, He teaching us about His character, about what He does and how He functions, from the very beginning!

In the phrase "let us make man in our image," the word *image* is not referring to the shape of His ears, mouth and nose; that idea of image

31

is Greek. *Image* is actually referring to God's function and character. "Let us make man after our [function and character]." That Hebraic application changes everything. Why was man created? Our purpose is not just to worship God, but to do what God does! Man was created in God's image, in His function, and in His character. We are to function like God functions. Genesis 1:27 means then that "God filled man with his own character."

But that also leaves us with the question: what does God do? There are so many answers to that question. The answer has to do with the word *filled*.

"FILLED"

To this point in the Torah, Genesis 2, what has God done that we should also do? Well, He created the heavens and the earth, light, introduced a concept of time, made the firmament, gathered the waters, and brought forth dry land, commanded grasses and trees to grow on that land, created the sun, moon and stars, made creatures of the sea, the air and land, and then He made man to function like He does. Doing what God does seems like a pretty tall order!

The word "created" from Genesis 1:1, is in Hebrew "*bara.*" "God *bara* the heavens and earth" has an alternate meaning that tends to get left behind, and it is much more functional in its description. *Bara* literally means "to make fat" or "to fill something" (Strong's #1254a and 1254b).[1] Our translation of the word "created" is a Greek-minded word which gives us the impression that God created the earth out of nothing. I have to be honest and say that I'm still mulling this over: the concept that God *filled* the earth instead of "created something out of nothing in six days." So, I am just telling you what it says in Hebrew.

The same word *bara* is used in I Samuel 2:29 and I Samuel 12:17. The root of *bara* is *bar* and it means grain. The first verse translates *bara* as "to make yourselves fat." The second mention of *bara* in Samuel is translated "grain," from "grain harvest." So think functionally: if we wanted to fatten a calf we would feed it grain. It literally means "to fill up" So in Hebrew the word *bara* has nothing to do with making something out of nothing, but to do with filling something up.

If we re-read the entire Creation story with "to make fat" or "to fill something" in mind, it becomes much easier to follow based on some of our non-hokey science findings on the age of the earth. God has Earth and He is filling it out day by day, and He has not stopped filling it. He fills us with His spirit day after day. *Bara* also speaks to man's function: we are to *fill* the earth, not just with the next generations, but fill the earth with life, with order (out of disorder that came with the Fall). I am a creationist. I believe God made it all *and* filled it up. I am telling you this so that you will dig your own wells. No matter how long you have been studying the Bible, there is always more to discover in God and His Word. God is good at not fitting in the box.

In addition, when God proclaimed something was *tov*, in the Hebrew that means it is fully functioning as it is supposed to do. It is functioning like a well-oiled machine working according to its created purpose, working in order. So when God sees the trees and birds and animals and calls them good, He's not saying, "Thumbs up, Self, that's really nice work!" He is saying "This is functional and in order as I designed it." Conversely, when God says something is evil, He is not saying it is demonic; He is saying it is dysfunctional or out of order. It is still working, but it's got issues…think of a dysfunctional family. It is still a family, and you can get by with it, especially if it is

33

all you have, but it is not working the way God intended family to function.

Expanding on the family example, whether they are believers in Jesus or not: think of a young couple who marries with an ideal of what their life and family will be like. As years go by, mistakes are made, forgiveness cannot be found, offenses arise over and over. Children are added to this family adding more stress to the mess. People get tired, lazy and unintentional about loving one another. One of the couple might leave, or become abusive; or the mess might be as simple as not being as loving and harmonious as they had planned to be in their family life from the beginning. This family is in dysfunction. They are still living and going about their day to day existence, still working, still experiencing happiness. Life goes on. But they are not living according to the ideal plan, and accordingly, they are living in dysfunction.

That is the difference between function and dysfunction. Dysfunction works, it just wobbles a little (or a lot). Our world is now in dysfunction because of sin. The key is that it is still functioning, just not the way the Father intended.

This idea of function and order is why when people need to clear their heads, they want to go for a walk or take a hike, smell the flowers. People go back to nature. What is happening is that people need to walk into something that is functioning the way God intended. Nature is where creation is functioning in order. As we are in that place of order, our spirits are connecting to that and coming into order too. Think of the Grand Canyon, the ocean, or Niagara Falls. What do people think about when we behold these things? How big God is, how small we are. That is our spirit coming into order from disorder.

Even unbelievers' feel regenerated into better order from God's order in nature, though they do not recognize it as coming from God.

The Tree of Knowledge of Good (*tov*) and Evil (*ra*) is a mistranslation. It should be understood as function and dysfunction. In the same way there is no darkness, only the absence of light, there is no evil, only the absence (or dysfunction) of God's perfect function. However, there are greatly varying degrees of dysfunction that can be seen in comparing the dysfunction of a disobedient child to the dysfunction of the Holocaust. God wanted to shield mankind from ever knowing about dysfunction by telling Adam and Even not to eat of the Tree of Function and Dysfunction. How kind He is.

After God's perfect filling of the earth of Genesis 1 and 2, Satan introduced dysfunction to God's world. It is not as if everything is now destroyed and not working at all, but it is off kilter, off the mark. Life still plods along, but it is dysfunctional, not running exactly according to the function God made it for.

All that and it's just the first couple verses of Genesis. Makes you think... "Hmm, I gotta start reading the Bible; this is really good stuff!" Take the revelation the Lord gives you through these meanings and ask Him about them, relationship and conversation is the intention of the Torah (the function); it is where life is.

HEBREW ALEF-BET

As we dig into the entomology of Hebrew words, it might be helpful to use the following chart as a reference for the letters and their sounds and equivalent English letters.

Alef	א	vowel sounds
Bet	ב/בּ	B/V
Gimmel	ג	G
Dalet	ד	D
Hey	ה	H
Vav	ו	V /vowel sound
Zayin	ז	Z
Chet	ח	Ch guttural
Tet	ט	T
Yod	י	Y / I
Kof (Kofsofit)	ך כ/כּ	K or ch
Lamed	ל	L
Mem (Memsofit)	ם מ	M, soft m
Nun (Nunsofit)	ן נ	N, soft n
Samech	ס	S
Ayin	ע	Vowel sound
Pey (Peysofit)	ף פ/פּ	P/f
Tsadi (Tsadisofit)	ץ צ	Ts/Z
Kuf	ק	Q/K
Resh	ר	R
Shen	שׁ/שׂ	S/ Sh
Tav	ת	T

WAYWARD THINKING

There are a couple of things that have been misunderstood in our western/Greek way of thinking. One of the most important bit of thinking that has been lost in our movement to think Greek, is our Christian understanding of the word *holy*.

The Hebrew word *kadosh* is translated "holy" in English Bibles. In the Hebraic world and language, *holy* does not mean what we think it does. It does not mean pure and good and white and pious and clean and untouchable. It is a lot simpler than that. Holiness is not righteousness; that's why it is a different word.

"A principle in Hebrew is that all Hebrew words are related through their spelling. Different words using the very same letters have connections in meanings. We find a

> ### A NOTE ON HEBREW SPELLING
>
> Written Hebrew words are spelled only with consonants. There are no vowels. However, vowel sounds are added in spoken/read Hebrew. When words are transliterated to English, usually vowels are added to distinguish words from each other. The word or string of Hebrew consonants is called the *shoresh*.
>
> Very simply, the connections between (sometimes seemingly different) concepts in Hebrew come from shared order of letters in their *shoresh* spelling. It was intentional.

very interesting connection concerning the word *holy* in the story of Judah, the son of Jacob, who saw his daughter-in-law wearing a veil, disguised as a harlot. The Torah relates that he thought that she was a '*kadasha*' (see Genesis 38:21). The word for a harlot in Hebrew is '*kadasha*' (as found in Deuteronomy 23:17-18) and the word for holiness is '*kadusha*'."[1]

> **Leviticus 11:45** For I am the LORD who brings you up and out of the land of Egypt, to be your God. You shall therefore be holy; for I am holy. (שׁוֹדָק *kadash*)

> **Genesis 38:21** Then he asked the men of that place, saying, "Where is the harlot (הַקְּדֵשָׁה *kadasha*) who *was* openly by the roadside?" And they said, "There was no harlot in this *place.*"

> **Deuteronomy 23:17-18** (NIV) No Israelite man or woman is to become a shrine prostitute. (*Kadasha*) [18] You must not bring the earnings of a female prostitute (*Kadasha*) or of a male prostitute (*Kadasha*) into the house of the LORD your God to pay any vow, because the LORD your God detests them both. (Italics mine).

This blew my mind. How could the same pattern of letters be used to refer to both God and prostitution? They are opposites. Actually, it is our idea of "holy" that is off. *Holy* simply means "set apart for a specific purpose."

The Hebrew root word used for temple prostitutes is the same word (*Kodash*) used in scripture for *holy*. It doesn't mean pure and clean. Holy simply means to be set apart for a specific purpose. Have you worked in the food industry where you had different pitchers for tea or soda or water? The water pitcher can *only* be used for water. By definition those water pitcher are holy. They are set aside for a specific purpose. Your Bible reading should be changed forever now!

Let's re-examine a couple of "holy" scriptures (bold added):

> **Exodus 19:5-6** [5] Now if you obey me fully and keep my covenant, then out of all nations you will be my treasured possession. Although the whole earth is mine, you will be for me a kingdom of priests and a **holy** nation.' These are the words you are to speak to the Israelites."

> **Leviticus 20:26-27**: "Do not defile yourselves by any animal or bird or anything that moves along the

ground—those that I have set apart as unclean for you.
[26] You are to be **holy** to me because I, the LORD, am **holy**, and I have set you apart from the nations to be my own."

God is spelling out that Israel is to be a nation "set apart (from all other nations) for a specific purpose." It has nothing to do with outward actions, or righteousness, it has to do with being chosen for a specific purpose. They are a "water pitcher." But what is their purpose? God's intention with Israel is to make them a light to the nations that are wrapped in the darkness of sin and their own way of thinking, to show the nations there is another way. Israel, the nation/people, are not clean and pure and without sin themselves, instead, they are set aside for a specific purpose. They are a critical part of the plan of God that is unfolding through the ages, the goal of which is to reconcile all men, or as many as who will receive Him, to God, that life could be life it was meant to be, as it was in the beginning. God wants to bring man back into function!

So as described in Revelation 4:8 when the four living creatures stand around the throne crying "Holy, holy, holy is the Lord God Almighty! Who was and is and is to come." They are saying in essence, "You are set apart from all else! How unlike any other are you! There is no one like You! No one could make the decisions you make!"[12]

Does this Hebraic explanation change the way we Christians read things? The priest's clothing and the articles in the tabernacle made for sacrifice are called holy, meaning that they are set aside for a special purpose and not to be used for everyday purposes. They are not attributed with any spooky aura. They themselves are not clean and pure. They are just set apart.

SINCE WE ARE GRAFTED INTO ISRAEL, WHAT DOES "HOLY" MEAN FOR CHRISTIANS?

Most importantly, we take nothing away from Israel's holiness, their set-apartness! They are not diminished in any way. Israel is *added to* by Christians as we are grafted into their holiness. We should live in such a way as to be obviously set apart from the world, not blend in. Christians are set apart for their own specific purpose too. Israel's purpose is to be a light to the nations (Isaiah 49:6; Luke 2:32), to draw them to God; the Church's purpose is to be a light to Israel, to support her in her calling (Yeah, I know that's not what you learned in Sunday School), and show her (through provoking jealousy as taught in Romans 11:11) the way to her Messiah. The word light is used often in scripture to refer to "truth." The only way the Gentiles will be able to provoke Israel i=to jealousy is through truth and love.

There are not two separate Covenants for Israel and the Church. It is one, just as we are one new man. The one new man Paul describes in Ephesians 2:15 is the Jew and believing Gentile functioning as one. There are not separate salvation plans for Israel and the Church. Jesus was the Jewish Messiah and His death and resurrection opened the invitation to Gentiles to come to the God of Israel. That is not saying we become Jewish (nor should we act or dress like Israelis).

HEBREW MEANING OF "RIGHTEOUS"

The word *righteous,* or *tzadik* in Hebrew, literally means "to be straight." *Tzadik* refers not to "walking in a line" but "walking in a right path or trail." Or "to continue on the path that God laid out," (i.e. the Torah). *Unrighteous* literally means "crooked" or "walking on a crooked path" so you have to "repent" (turn around 180 degrees and get on the straight path).

Many people confuse *holy* and *righteous*. Both Israel and the Church are called to be both!

HEBREW MEANING OF "TORAH"

First, let's go back to the scripture itself to see what the Torah asserts itself to be.

> **Psalm 119:105:** Your word (Torah) is a lamp unto my feet and a light unto my path.

> **Psalm 19:7-11** NKJV
> The law (Torah) of the LORD *is* perfect, converting the soul; the testimony of the LORD *is* sure, making wise the simple;
> [8] The statutes of the LORD *are* right, rejoicing the heart; The commandment of the LORD *is* pure, enlightening the eyes; [9] The fear of the LORD *is* clean, enduring forever; the judgments of the LORD *are* true *and* righteous altogether.
> [10] More to be desired *are they* than gold, Yea, than much fine gold; sweeter also than honey and the honeycomb.
> [11] Moreover by them Your servant is warned, *And* in keeping them *there is* great reward.

"The Torah is perfect, restoring our souls," really? That is an awfully big claim. Boaz Michael[3] brings up this question in his blog, "(I)sn't Jesus the restorer of our souls, rather than the Torah? Maybe King David said this because he didn't know Jesus. On the other hand, maybe it only seems misguided to us because we don't understand the Torah." Usually *Torah* is defined as "law" but we Western/Greek thinkers have a wrong concept attached to the scriptures as a result of this inadequate translation. We tend to think of *law* as a rigid line drawn in the sand, that if you step over the line, or break the law, you go to jail. In America, because of our fiercely independent nature, we have almost a revolting feeling associated with *law*. From our movies to our songs, our culture makes fun of the law and the police or other governmental authorities designed to keep the peace, or enforce the law. We take those feelings to our Bibles as we read about the law there.

To begin our study of this Hebrew word, the actual concept of Torah is from the field of archery. The root word of Torah, *yarah*, means "to take aim, to shoot" like when an archer aims his arrow to shoot a target.[12] The function of Torah is to hit the mark (the target of a person's heart). The opposite of hitting the mark, is missing the mark. That has a Hebrew word too, *hata*. *Hata* is often translated into English as the word *sin*. So sin is "missing the mark."

The word *yarah* also has a hidden meaning of "teach."[6] Proverbs 6:23 says "The commandment is a lamp, and the law a light; Reproofs of instruction are the way of life." This verse sounds very similar to Psalm 119:105 (above). This concept of light as found in the words *lamp* and *light* is encompassed in the Hebrew word *ore*. It seems to be another one of those play-on-words that God enjoys: we can hear it if we say it aloud: *Ore, Torah*. There is a word-sound-concept connection between light and Torah.

Another Hebrew word that comes from the Hebrew root word of *yarah* is *moreh*. Can you hear the connection from this root word? *yarah, moreh, Torah, ore*? The word *moreh* (Strong's: 4175) encompasses both the concepts of an archer and a teacher, meaning that *Moreh* is a person.

According to the Jewsandjoes.com author, Hanok, "Ultimately, the word *Torah*, could be defined as and/or perceived as this: the Light (*ore*) which the Teacher (*Moreh*) casts in a direction (*yarah*) for us to walk in (*halak*)."[6] Isn't that beautiful? A more simple root meaning of *Torah* can be translated as this: "a set of instructions to stay on the trail."

The people of Israel were given this "set of instructions to stay on the trail" as a code of conduct that, if they followed it, would set up the Jewish people to be successful in all they do. Messianic songwriter Ted Pearce says, "The Torah was given through Moses by the hand of God as the Constitution of a new nation, comprised of former-slaves leaving Egypt. It is the very first revelation of God's character and the central foundation of all covenants, including the "New" one mentioned first in Jeremiah 31:31."[14]

When we factor in John 1:1, "In the beginning was the Word and the Word was with God and the Word was God," and we easily accept that Jesus was the Word, what Word are they talking about? The Torah. Jesus was the Torah? What a concept!

The Torah is far more than the unbending law. It is a standard of measurement, a righteousness to live up to. Not that following Torah will provide salvation; God never intended that. The Torah sets before people righteousness and unrighteousness, function and dysfunction, black and white; God sets before people a choice. Righteousness cannot be based on what *feels* right or wrong to me. The Torah clearly lays it out; people cannot claim right is subjective. There is no excuse; we all fall short. (Romans 3:23).

There is even a concept in Judaism for one who does manage to keep the whole law. He still cannot be perfect because he will be proud that he has kept the whole law and does not need a savior. Therefore in being perfect, he has sinned. God thinks of everything!

HEBREW MEANING OF "SHALOM"
Shalom (Strong's: 7965) comes from the Hebrew word *shalam* (Strong's: 7999) which means "completeness" or "to be in health and prosperity." Shalom is usually translated "peace." It is used in

greetings and farewells as well as in scripture. In the west, we tend to think of peace in one of three ways: 1. some hippy version of "peace-out, bro," 2. plain, simple quietness, or 3. a lack of war. You might even conjure up a dove with an olive branch if you've been in Christian circles for a while. But again the translation has lost much of its Hebraic richness. There is more to shalom than just peace. It refers to being made safe in body, mind or estate, to being complete, to being well, happy and friendly. Shalom refers an inner completeness and wholeness. When used as a greeting or farewell it functions as a blessing over people, as if you are saying, "May you dwell in inner peace." Take a deep breath and let that shalom soak into your spirit.

In Isaiah 9:6, the Messiah is referred to as the "Sar Shalom." *Sar* (Strong's: 8269) means a male prince, leader, ruler, or captain. "The Prince of Inner Completeness" is a perfect description of Yeshua.

When Jesus' birth was announced in the heavens and the angels sang, "Glory to God in the highest and on earth peace, good will toward men" (Luke 2:14), they used the word *shalom*. The shalom (inner completeness) from heaven is now available on earth. The Kingdom of God is coming, and Jesus is the "first installment!"

PRAY FOR THE PEACE (SHALOM) OF JERUSALEM [4]
In Psalm 122:6-7 we are admonished to "Pray for the peace of Jerusalem: may they prosper who love you. Peace be within your walls, prosperity within your palaces." That first phrase transliterated from Hebrew sounds like "sha'alu shalom yerushalaim" which is generally translated "pray for the peace of Jerusalem." It is beautiful in itself—and fits well on a bumper sticker. But there is a deeper meaning we are missing.

Sha'alu comes from the root word *sha'al* (Strong's: 7592) which means to earnestly inquire, or to make request. The extra *u* on the end of sha'al designates that the subject of this verb is plural.

Shalom we covered above, and *yerushalaim* (Strong's: 3389) is a combination of two words: *Yeru* which means "to teach" and *shalam*, which is the same root we covered with shalom.

Therefore putting all these meanings together, "The full Hebraic understanding of this verse is 'All of you make a request that the ones who teach shalom/completeness will be given health and prosperity.'"[4] That understanding puts whole new spin of praying for Jerusalem. We are not responsible to pray that a city will not be at war, but that the ones who teach us about the inner completeness only found in God will be given health and prosperity. It also implies that we should be learning from the Jewish people about God's shalom.

WHAT DOES *ISRAEL* MEAN?[5]

In most definitions you will see Israel defined as "struggles/wrestles with God" or "prince with God." For Jacob whose name was changed to Israel, the meaning "prince with God" is a huge step up from the previous name he had been living with. Jacob means "supplanter," with an expanded meaning of "a tricky cheater on his own against the world".

Here is the etymology of *Israel*. Israel is a combination of two Hebrew words: *Yisra* and *el*. You probably already know that *el* means God. It is part of the same root word from which *Elohim* comes. *Yisra* is derived from the root word *sar* meaning "Prince." This is where the meaning of "prince with God" comes from and Jacob's destiny changed dramatically with his new name.

But wait, there's more! Let's break down the individual roots in Israel.[5]

45

Israel in Hebrew is spelled: yod, shen, resh, alef, lamed. The yod (I or Y sound) is a word unto itself. It means *he*. The next two letters together [shen (S) and resh (R)] form the word SaR. It designates a *ruler* or *prince*, but it also means "to turn the head." Several other root words derived from SaR are:

1. *ASaR* (alef, shen, resh) which means "a yoke which turns the head of the ox."

2. *SaYaR* (shen, yod, resh) which means "a fishhook which turns the head of a fish."

3. *YaSaR* (yod, shen, resh) which means "to discipline as you turn the head," or "change the direction of the one you discipline."

4. *SaHaR* (shen, chet, resh) which means "to turn around."

The last two letters in *Israel* are alef and lamed which together form the word *el*, meaning "God." When taken as a whole these three root words mean: "he turns the head of God." Isn't that exactly what Israel does? Israel is called the apple of God's eye (Deuteronomy 32:10 & Zechariah 2:8). Abram changed God's mind about destroying Sodom if they could find 10 righteous people. Moses caused God to spare the people of Israel after the golden calf incident.

MORE ON HEBREW VOWEL SOUNDS

A small letter inserted into a Hebrew word is a vowel added for ease of English readers. Only the capitalized consonant sounds are present in the Hebrew *shoresh*. Vowel sounds are present even when the *shoresh* spelling does not show it.

HIDDEN IN THE NAME *ISRAEL*[13]

Here is an extra bit of fun that can be found in the name *Israel*. Have you noticed that the first letter of each of the names of the patriarchs and their wives are contained in the name *Israel* in Hebrew?

Yod—Isaac (Yitchak), Jacob (Ya'acov)

Shen—Sarah

Resh—Rachel, Rebekah (Rivkah)

Alef—Abraham (Avraham)

Lamed—ELohim (God)

THE HEBREW WORD/NAME MOSHEH (MOSES)[7]

The Hebrew spelling of Mosheh or Moses is mem, shen, hey. Exodus 2:10 says Moses was named by the daughter of the pharaoh, because she drew him out of the water. According to Exodus 2:6 the woman knew the child was a Hebrew. The name *Moses* on the surface means "drawn out" even in the footnotes of your Bible. But there is a deeper meaning embedded that can be found by breaking down the words within his name.

There are two words that make up this name: Mi and SeH. *Mi* means "from" and *SeH* means "the lamb." Together the meaning becomes *from the lamb.*

Wasn't Moses a gift from Jesus (the Lamb) to the Hebrew people to free them from slavery? Moses' destiny was written in his name...even a name given to him by a pagan. And it was in Moses' lifetime that the Passover lamb became part of the Israelite-Hebrew culture for the rest of time. Moses was the person God chose to institute His Feast of the Passover during which every year the Jews remember the lamb who foreshadowed the coming Lamb: Messiah Yeshua.

Something interesting beyond that: If you spell Mosheh backward in Hebrew it is hey, shen, mem. *HaSheM,* which is also a word. It means *The Name.* This word is used daily in Hebrew. *HaShem* is what Jews call God in the vernacular, because His name is too holy to pronounce or write. (You've probably seen writings where they leave out the vowels or add a dash to avoid spelling God, such as: G-d or L-rd.) Mosheh spelled backward is HaShem. That's neat, but what does it mean?

47

The meaning "is as simple as this: Moses was sent *from the lamb* to proclaim *The Name* of the One God to the world. Moses and Torah point the way." [7]

AN ABSTRACT THOUGHT IN HEBREW: "BLESSING" [9]

Despite abstract thinking or appearance-based thought being more Greek in origin, it is not as if the Hebrews had no abstract kind of thinking even in their most ancient days. They did, and the word for *blessing* is an example.

The English word "blessing" is translated from the Hebrew word *berakah*. The root word of *berakah* is spelled bet, resh, kaph. When used as a noun it is pronounced *berek*. It means knee or the part of the body that bends. When used as a verb it is pronounced *barak* and it means "to kneel." When other letters are added to the root word it changes the meaning slightly, though all meanings are related to each other through the shoresh. When the letter chet is added, the word becomes berakah. According to Brenner, "This word (*berakah*,) is a gift or present and is related to the root through the idea of bending down to the knee and presenting a gift to another."[9]

Here is **Genesis 27:38** translated in KJV: "And Esau said unto his father, Hast thou but one blessing (*berakah*), my father? bless (*barak*) me, even me also..."

Brenner gives a more literal translation: "And Esau said unto his father, Hast thou but one **gift** (berakah), my father? **Kneel down and present me a gift** (barak), even me also..." [9] (emphasis his).

In Hebrew even the abstract links back to concrete terms and picture-thoughts, whereas Greek thoughts remain abstract. In Hebraic thinking a blessing is any thing or action, given out of respect for another.

THE SIGN PILATE FIXED TO THE CROSS

John 19:19 Pilate had a notice prepared and fastened to the cross. It read: JESUS OF NAZARETH, THE KING OF THE JEWS.

In Hebrew, Pilate's sign would have read "Yeshua Ha'nozti V'melach Ha'yehudim." Each first letter of a Hebrew word was bolded, so the sign's bolded letters spelled a word of their own. The bold letters on Pilate's sign were yod, hey, vav, hey.

Those letters spell the tetragrammaton which is the holy, unspeakable name of God: *Yahweh (Jehovah)!* It would have been obvious to any Hebrew speaker looking at it. The sign over Jesus head as He hung on the cross said, "God"! In the specific holy name they were not supposed to say, much less proclaim it over a man dying saying He is God! It was for this reason that the people wanted the sign changed to say "Jesus of Nazareth, who says he is the king of the Jews." The bolded first letters would have been different so that God's holy name would not be associated with Yeshua.

> ### HEBREW WORD BREAKS
> In Hebrew there is no distinction between capital or small letters like we have in English. In ancient days there was neither punctuation marks nor spacing between words. So you can imagine how difficult a translator's job is. The only distinguishing mark in Hebrew is that a thicker reed was used on each first letter of a word. Similar to bold font. If we did this in English is would look like this: **READABLEBUTDIFFI CULT.**

Several sources discount this name on the sign because the gospels each present a different wording.[2] However, of all four gospel writers, John was the only one present at the cross, therefore his gospel would seem to be the most reliable source for the exact wording on the sign. Even if it wasn't written, the idea that it *could* have been, is amazing!

"LEGION"[11]

Remember the story about when Jesus cast the demons out of the Gadarene man (Mark 5 & Luke 8)? Here is a little funny that you probably missed since not many people speak Greek *and* Hebrew. When Jesus asked the name of the demon tormenting the man (the only time in scripture this is done, by the way), the demon answered. Those people who spoke Greek and were standing around would have heard, "Legion, because we are many." A legion in the Greek world was an army corps. Those people who were present and were Hebrew speakers would have heard "*Leshon.*" (Hear how they sound nearly identical?) *Leshon* in Hebrew means "accuser or slanderer." Isn't it interesting how this demon, as he calls himself, describes his function.

That is what Hebrew words and thought processes do, describe function.

END NOTES

1. Lazerson, Avi. (n.d.) Holiness and Judaism. *Jewish Magazine*. Retrieved Jan 31, 2012 from http://jewishmag.com/39mag/holy/holy.htm

2. Here is an interesting discussion if you want more on the tetragramaton written above Jesus' cross: http://theosophical.wordpress.com/2011/04/27/did-the-accusation-above-jesus%E2%80%99-cross-form-an-acrostic-spelling-%E2%80%9Cyhwh%E2%80%9D/

3. Boaz Michael's blog on the topic of Torah can be accessed at http://ffoz.org/blogs/2009/10/torah_does_not_mean_law.html

4. Notes on Pray for the Peace of Jerusalem section and the quote were retrieved December 7, 2012 from http://www.ancient-hebrew.org/1_faqs_learnhebrew.html

5. Notes on "Israel" meaning retrieved April 28, 2013 from http://www.ancient-hebrew.org/1_faqs_vocabulary.html#israel1.

6. Hanok. (n.d.). The meaning of Torah as light. Retrieved April 30, 2013 from http://jewsandjoes.com/etymology-of-torah.html

7. Thoene, Brock and Thoene, Bodie. 2001. *Jerusalem's Heart*. Penguin Group. New York. p. 219-220.

8. An online course in ancient Hebrew can be found here: http://education.ancient-hebrew.org/index.html

9. Info on the word Blessing came from Jeff A. Benner's research retrieved May 30, 2013 from http://www.ancient-hebrew.org/thelivingwords/bless.pdf

10. Cantor, Ron. 2013. *Identity Theft*. Destiny Image.

11. Thoene, Bodie and Thoene, Brock. 2004. *Third Watch*. Tyndall House Publishers, Wheaton, Illinois. Pg xvi.

12. Hershey, Doug. Spring 2011. Jesus in the Torah Seminar. Richmond, VA RIHOP

13. Withers, Diane. 2007. Israel 101 Course at Church of the Highlands, small groups. Birmingham, AL.

14. Pearce, Ted. 2014. Facebook status update. Issue #3 para 6 Retrieved April 30, 2014 from https://www.facebook.com/#!/ted.pearce.18?fref=ts

3

FINDING JESUS IN GENESIS 5

FINDING JESUS IN GOD'S HEART: THE TORAH

God's heart for us inundates the scripture. From the stories of people's experience to the prophetic pictures He paints to the individual words and even the very intricate detail in the order of the words He chose.

HEART

The first word of the Torah in Genesis 1:1 in Hebrew is *Bersheet* which means "in the beginning." The first letter of that Hebrew word is a bet. The very last word in the Torah in Deuteronomy is *"Yisrael"* or Israel, which ends in the Hebrew letter lamed. If you combine those two letters, bet and lamed, you get the Hebrew word *"lev."* In Hebrew, *lev* means *heart.* So from the very first letter of the Torah to the very last letter, the Torah encompasses God's heart. It is almost like God is saying: "This is my heart for you! I love you and I want you to succeed, so I am giving you my heart, my Word to cause that

53

to happen." The Torah is God's heart, even down to the letter. It is communicating God's heart. Everything in it points to Jesus!

Jesus in the Torah: The 1000 Years' Prophecy

When God names people it is not merely a way to get their attention. As we learned in chapter two, in Hebraic thinking names have to do with function, not appearance. A name has to do with character and destiny. Every time we call someone's name we are calling out their destiny. It is especially obvious when God changes a name like Abram to Abraham and Jacob to Israel. Abram, means "exalted father" but God had more in mind for this man than that, God renamed him "Abraham" meaning "father of many nations" and out of Abraham has come the modern nations of Israel, Jordan, Iraq, Iran, Saudi Arabia, Lebanon, Syria and more. Not Egypt though, and that will be important to remember later. (Much more on names is covered in chapter 12)

If the Torah is God's heart, and Jesus is God's heart, then we should be able to find Jesus in the Torah. Or at least characteristics we recognize as Jesus. Let's look at Genesis 5, one of the most obscure who-begat-whom genealogy chapters, and see if we can find Him there. Like me you may have skipped over that part because it was boring. But everything in scripture is there for a reason. It is God's heart and He doesn't need to fill space! Everything in the Torah points to Jesus. It might be hidden at first, but God loves to reveal Himself.

Genealogy [2] of Genesis 5

We can learn a lot about God and His character and Jesus from genealogical record in Genesis 5 because names speak of function and character and *destiny*. So we'll look at the first 10 generations, Adam to Noah, which covered over 1600 years and is considered the first "age" of the earth.

ADAM means "man from the Earth" because he was formed from the earth and one of his primary responsibilities was to take care of the earth. His call did not change after being kicked out of the garden, even though it was now dysfunctional. It was dysfunctional because the garden and life were no longer functioning as God intended.

Both inside and outside of the garden, Adam's call was to cultivate the ground. The difference is that God never intended for Adam to cultivate the ground outside the place of pleasure (garden). The gifts and call of the Lord are not changing or withdrawn! Hmm, that sounds kind of "New Testament" (I wonder where the New Testament got it?).

SETH means "to set something in place" or "appoint something." In Hebrew it literally means "the place of where you sit." Because Cain killed Able, Seth was the third born child, but was named Seth, because he was "set in place" of the others. They looked at it as God reestablishing the line.

ENOSH means "mortal, mortality" or "man's sickness or weakness." Genesis 4:26-27 says "then men began to call on the name of the Lord." There was something going on in the earth during the time of Enosh's birth that Seth named him "man's sickness or man's weakness." Then afterward men began to call on the name of the Lord.

CAINAN means "to make a nest or dwelling place." This name is different from the land of Canaan. Cainan's "nest" is like a mother

55

bird that goes about gathering twigs and stuff to make a place for her young to be comfortable.

MAHALALEL comes from a combination of two words *Mahalal* and *El*. As we discussed earlier, El refers to "God," but *mahalal* means to shine or to praise. *Hallel* is often translated "to praise." The functional Hebrew picture created by this string of Hebrew words actually refers to "gazing at something that is bright or shining." Together, Mahalalel means "the shining one of God" or "the praise of God."

JARED means "to go down" or "to descend." The Hebrew word-function picture literally refers to a ruler or a father who goes in to a tent and sits on the floor, as in when he plays with his children.

ENOCH means "to dedicate." This word *dedicate* is not like a baby dedication. It refers to "beginning to use something new by being taught or trained." Think of it like someone who is extra good at sports or art being dedicated. They've been doing something through training and are now functioning at a level of excellence where they can train others.

Enoch is spoken of elsewhere in the Bible.

> **Jude 1:14-15** Now Enoch, the seventh from Adam, prophesied about these men also, saying, "Behold, the Lord comes with ten thousands of His saints, [15]to execute judgment on all, to convict all who are ungodly among them of all their ungodly deeds which they have committed in an ungodly way, and of all the harsh things which ungodly sinners have spoken against Him."

Now that sounds like someone who is dedicated! Enoch is on a whole other level from everyone else. He is speaking like he is seeing it happen live, "the Lord came with many thousands of his holy ones to execute judgment!" That sounds prophetic, like the end of days.

We see in Genesis 5:24 that "Enoch walked with God and then was not, for God took him." And in Hebrews 11:5 "Enoch was taken up so he would not see death." Enoch is the seventh generation. Only Adam had died yet. But people are starting to understand death now. However, Enoch was taken up, he did not die. Enoch's way of passing is the way it was intended before mankind sinned. Apparently Enoch was so dedicated to the Lord that not only was he having wild prophetic experiences, but he understood the idea of godly and ungodly and righteous and unrighteous, function and dysfunction. He was so zoned in with God that he returned to the lifestyle of the garden so much so, that he never saw death. God must have been thinking, *This guy is really getting it; I'm taking him with Me!*

METHUSELAH is derived from a combination of three words: Met-U-Shalah. *Met* (means "death") *U* (makes the death mean "his death") and *Shalah* (means "to send something or to bring something"). Combined then, Methuselah means "his death shall bring." This is a prophetic name. (really!? what an awful name for your kid!) But remember who named him: his dad was Enoch. Enoch was living at a whole other level, seeing events at the end of the ages. So what happened at this man's death? Methushelah died in 1656 BC, the year of the flood is also 1656! The year Methuselah died is the year of the flood. Um…his death shall bring?!

Not only that, but also, Methuselah is the longest living man, 969 years, so just by God extending his life, He is extending mercy to the rest of the family. By the time Methuselah died, even his own son Lamech, was dead. By the time the flood came, everyone else in Noah's family had already passed away. Isn't that God's mercy! He extends a life, because "his death will bring," and that displays God's heart toward people. He wants to give people every chance to get back in line with God. God's great mercy was to delay the flood! Methuselah's dad knew that something big was coming the year his son died. And so it was God's mercy that kept Methuselah alive longer than anyone else, even his own son!

LAMECH means "to be low" or "despairing."

NOAH means "to bring rest or comfort." *Noah* is like a shepherd who leads his sheep to a place of quiet, outside of burdens, and the name also encompasses an aspect of leadership within it. Lamech named him Noah saying, "This is the one who will give us rest from our work and from the toils of our hands, arising from the ground which the Lord has cursed" (Genesis 5:29).

This becomes a 1600 year long prophecy just by following the meanings of their names, the men's functions and destiny. Remember each of these names is function of who they are. They fulfilled in their generation what their names meant. But do you see Jesus yet?

When all these men are lined up in the order of their birth, this is what their names say: a man from the earth was set in place because of man's weakness and sickness or mortality. To make a nest, the shining one of God descended or came down, dedicating himself or teaching others that his death will bring the low (or those who work and toil), to rest. Do you see Jesus now?

We will line up all these men with their name's meaning again:
Adam: means "man" but there is also a word play (*adamah*) meaning earth.
Seth: means "appointed" sounds like the Hebrew word for "to give"

Enosh: means "human being" or "mortal and frail" (in root words) denoting that during Enosh's lifetime is when human being first began to defile the name of the Lord

Cainan or Kenan: means "possession"

Mahalalel: means "praise of God"

Jared: means (descent) or to descend or "shall come down"

Enoch: means "dedicated" "teaching or commencement"

Methuselah: sounds like the Hebrew words for *his death brings.* Alternate meaning is "when he is dead it shall be sent"

Lamech: means "to be low or despairing"

Noah: means "to bring rest or comfort"

The first ten generations of people in the line of Jesus, became a prophetic word from God that He would send Jesus to us! And God was faithful to His word.

END NOTES

1. Information from Strong's Concordance on Hebrew words and meanings can be accessed at http://biblesuite.com/hebrew/1254b.htm

2. Genesis 5:3-32 is the entire text describing the generations and their years on the earth. It is interesting to note that for Adam's 930 years, mankind had already entered our eighth generation. For 56 years Adam through Lamech were alive together and could talk to each other and learn from each other. I would have loved to be around that campfire with Papa Adam recounting what it used to be like to walk with God in the cool of the day! And what it was like to lose that closeness.

4

JESUS FULFILLS THE TORAH AS A SIGN TO ISRAEL

Jesus said as recorded in Matthew 5:17 that he did not come to destroy the law but fulfill it. But what does that mean? How does one fulfill laws from the Torah about taking a spade with you when you need to relieve yourself or not eating ostrich? I can understand following it, but *fulfilling* it? In my western mind, I understand *prophecy* being fulfilled, but not law. Is there some connection there? Is there prophecy contained within the laws of the Covenant? Well, yes! What is meant by "fulfilling the law" is that Jesus followed it properly, the way God set it up to be followed. Every part of the Torah Jesus obeyed, both in the natural and in the spirit of the Law. And so it set Him apart from all others, as obedience to Torah was intended to do.

In obeying the Torah, Jesus became both a follower of the Torah and a prophecy. Everything written in the Bible up to when Yeshua appears on the scene in history is pointing forward to Jesus the Messiah (1st and 2nd coming), and everything written afterward points either back to Jesus and what He taught, or points to His coming again to fulfill the prophecies left undone.

When a human finally followed all the nuances of the Torah, it was to serve as an example to us, not as a "get-out-of-jail-free" card. There are so many problems with that mindset, it is hard to know where to begin setting the record straight. When Jesus fulfilled the laws of the Torah, it was supposed to serve as a sign to Israel. His obedience was to be a red glittery flag waving, shouting "Hey, look at this! Something special is going on here. No one else has ever done this before. This man must be God." But how did Jesus fulfilling the Torah play out in His daily life?

EMMAUS: THE BEST SERMON NEVER RECORDED

Remember the two men who walked on the road to Emmaus when Jesus appeared to them? Here is Luke's recount:

> **Luke 24:19-32** "What things?" he (newly resurrected Jesus) asked.
> "About Jesus of Nazareth," they replied. "He was a prophet, powerful in word and deed before God and all the people. 20 The chief priests and our rulers handed him over to be sentenced to death, and they crucified him; 21 but we had hoped that he was the one who was going to redeem Israel. And what is more, it is the third day since all this took place. 22 In addition, some of our women amazed us. They went to the tomb early this morning 23 but didn't find his body. They came and told us that they had seen a vision of angels, who said he was alive. 24 Then some of our

companions went to the tomb and found it just as the women had said, but they did not see Jesus."

25 He said to them, "How foolish you are, and how slow to believe all that the prophets have spoken! 26 Did not the Messiah have to suffer these things and then enter his glory?" 27 And <u>beginning with Moses and all the Prophets, he explained to them what was said in all the Scriptures concerning himself</u>...

30 When he was at the table with them, he took bread, gave thanks, broke it and began to give it to them. 31 Then their eyes were opened and they recognized him, and he disappeared from their sight. 32 They asked each other, <u>"Were not our hearts burning within us while he talked with us on the road and opened the Scriptures to us?"</u> (Emphasis mine)

What scriptures do you suppose Yeshua was uncovering for these men, especially in the Law of Moses? Here are some options Jesus had when explaining what the Scriptures said about Himself.

את

THE MESSIAH WOULD BE BOTH PRIEST AND KING[1]

According to David's prophecy about the coming Messiah in Psalm 110:4 "The LORD has sworn and will not change his mind: 'You are a priest forever, in the order of Melchizedek.'" We know this is a prophecy of the coming Messiah because no mere mortal could be a priest forever. We can go back to the Torah to meet Melchizedek and see what David's prophecy was referring to in this "order of Melchizedek."

Abram had gone to rescue his nephew Lot and was headed back to his camp via the King's Valley route. Genesis 14:18: "Then Melchizedek king of Salem brought out bread and wine. He was priest of God Most High." Melchiaedek was a prototype. He was the king of the land that would later become Jeru-Salem. Remember the connection between "salem" and "shalom" from chapter 2? By the name of the city he is ruling, this man is a king of inner peace. Looking at the Hebrew meaning of the name Melchizedek, we can also understand his function. *Melek* means king; *Tzadek* means righteous one. Putting that together into one name gives the meaning, "a righteous one who is king." In addition, when we meet Melchizedek, he is functioning and titled as "a priest of God Most High." He was the first priest and king combination.

David's prophecy of Psalm 110 depicts the coming Messiah as the same combination of priest and king of inner peace as found in the Torah. So how does Jesus fulfill this combination?

KING
Jesus' lineage is recorded back as far as Abraham in Matthew 1:1-17. It seems quite obvious that being born into the line of Judah and the family of David that Jesus would fulfill scripture of a promised Messiah who was in the kingly line. God promised David that a descendant of his would sit on the throne of Israel forever.

> **I Kings 9:5** I will establish your royal throne over Israel forever, as I promised David your father when I said, 'You shall never fail to have a successor on the throne of Israel.'

Because Jesus was born into this line of the house of David, He is eligible to be the Messiah as foretold. The priest part is a little trickier—but only if you don't study your Torah.

PRIEST
God ordained that the priestly line should come not only from the tribe of Levi, but also specifically from the family of Aaron's sons. At

first glance, it seems Jesus can only be a figurative high priest, because His genealogy is from Judah and David. We just established that from Matthew's record. But God doesn't lie or cheat. And we in the Greek/western mindset give Him credit for being far more figurative than He actually is. He is a practical God, who says what He means. He said the Messiah would be a priest also, so how could this happen?

We can go all the way back to the time of the Exodus from Egypt to see how God planted His little "loophole" of intention into the Torah. Because God saved all the firstborns in the house of Israel during the Passover of the Angel of Death, God says that all the firstborns of Israel belong to Him. (The first and best of *all* things belong to God!) Exodus 12 records what God plans to do:

> **Exodus 12:12-14** 'For I will pass through the land of Egypt on that night, and will strike all the firstborn in the land of Egypt, both man and beast; and against all the gods of Egypt I will execute judgment: I *am* the LORD. ¹³ Now the blood shall be a sign for you on the houses where you *are*. And when I see the blood, I will pass over you; and the plague shall not be on you to destroy *you* when I strike the land of Egypt.
> ¹⁴ 'So this day shall be to you a memorial; and you shall keep it as a feast to the LORD throughout your generations. You shall keep it as a feast by an everlasting ordinance.

Then more of God's plan is unveiled in
> **Exodus 13:1-2**, "The LORD said to Moses, 'Consecrate to me every firstborn male. The first offspring of every womb among the Israelites belongs to me, whether human or animal.'"

65

There doesn't seem to be any room for misunderstanding in those words. But what were the Israelites to do about fulfilling this instruction?

In **Exodus 13:11-15** this Law of the Firstborns becomes an everlasting ordinance.

> [11] After the LORD brings you into the land of the Canaanites and gives it to you, as he promised on oath to you and your ancestors, [12] you are to give over to the LORD the first offspring of every womb. All the firstborn males of your livestock belong to the LORD. [13] Redeem with a lamb every firstborn donkey, but if you do not redeem it, break its neck. Redeem every firstborn among your sons.
> [14] "In days to come, when your son asks you, 'What does this mean?' say to him, 'With a mighty hand the LORD brought us out of Egypt, out of the land of slavery. [15] When Pharaoh stubbornly refused to let us go, the LORD killed the firstborn of both people and animals in Egypt. This is why I sacrifice to the LORD the first male offspring of every womb and redeem each of my firstborn sons.'

RABBIT TRAIL
An added-for-free commentary on the current state of our nation and world: How many firstborn children have we aborted in the last 35 years? These children who belong to God from their foundation in life, their function of opening the womb, have been sacrificed to the god of convenience and selfishness instead of being dedicated to God and redeemed. Is it any wonder America as we knew it is falling apart? We have robbed God and murdered while claiming to be a nation founded on God! We are reaping the judgment we deserve. It is not ok.

The Lord receives the firstborn sons which belong to Him and gives them to the Levites. The parents of Israel are required to redeem their firstborn sons from the Levites. Here is how the Lord expressed it:

Numbers 18:14-16 "Everything in Israel that is devoted to the LORD is yours (Aaron). The first

offspring of every womb, both human and animal, that is offered to the LORD is yours. But <u>you must redeem every firstborn son</u> and every firstborn male of unclean animals. <u>When they are a month old, you must redeem them at the redemption price set at five shekels of silver,</u> according to the sanctuary shekel, which weighs twenty gerahs.

So every firstborn belongs to the Lord and is required to be redeemed with the price of five silver shekels.

JESUS IS BROUGHT TO THE TEMPLE.

Luke 2:22-24 & 39 When the time came for the purification rites required by the Law of Moses, Joseph and Mary took him to Jerusalem to present him to the Lord (as it is written in the Law of the Lord, "Every firstborn male is to be consecrated to the Lord"), and to offer a sacrifice in keeping with what is said in the Law of the Lord: "a pair of doves or two young pigeons..."
[39]When Joseph and Mary had done everything required by the Law of the Lord, they returned to Galilee to their own town of Nazareth.

Did you notice that Mary and Joseph paid the redemption price of a pair of young doves or pigeons instead of the five silver shekels? The Covenant makes provisions for poor people who cannot afford the price: **Leviticus 12:8** "But if she cannot afford a lamb, she is to bring two doves or two young pigeons, one for a burnt offering and the other for a sin offering." So Mary and Joseph fulfilled the Law by redeeming Jesus, the firstborn son of Mary's womb.

This fulfillment of the Torah law was a normal ritual among the people of Israel. So normal that two people (Simeon and Anna) who had both been promised that they would see the Messiah before they died, were hanging out at the temple. My guess is that they knew the

Messiah's parents would bring Him to the temple when He was 30 days old, and they would be sure to see (and recognize) Him if they were there checking out the babies. According to Luke 2:25-38, both Simeon and Anna recognized Jesus as Israel's Messiah when Mary and Joseph came to give Him to the Levitical priests and redeem Him back. The two prophets blessed Him and prophesied over Him in the hearing of all those present.

Jesus was already circumcised (an outward sign to show Jesus was a son of the Covenant) on the eighth day (Luke 2:21). This ritual of redeeming the firstborn occurred nearly three weeks later in a separate event.

WHY ARE FIRSTBORN SONS SO IMPORTANT TO GOD?

Firstborns are important not just because they are the ones God destroyed in Egypt. Originally God's plan was that the priests of Israel would be the firstborn male of every family. Every family in Israel would have a priest in their own home! It would facilitate family worship like no other religion could. Firstborns are usually natural leaders; they would add encouragement in their family to worship the God of Abraham, Isaac and Jacob. However the golden calf incident changed things. The Levites found favor with God. They were chosen from among the children of Israel to go into service at the Tabernacle, and later the Temple. Here is what changed things:

> **Exodus 32:25-29** Moses saw that the people were running wild and that Aaron had let them get out of control and so become a laughingstock to their enemies. 26 So he stood at the entrance to the camp and said, "Whoever is for the LORD, come to me." And all the Levites rallied to him.
> 27 Then he said to them, "This is what the LORD, the God of Israel, says: 'Each man strap a sword to his side. Go back and forth through the camp from one

68

end to the other, each killing his brother and friend and neighbor.'" [28] The Levites did as Moses commanded, and that day about three thousand of the people died. [29] Then Moses said, "You have been set apart to the LORD today, for you were against your own sons and brothers, and he has blessed you this day."

So because the Levites answered the question by rallying to Moses, effectively saying, "we believe the Lord and we're on His side," and then they followed through by going through the camp with swords and obeying the Lord's command, they became "chosen".

Numbers 8:14-19 describes God's change of plans from the firstborn to the Levites:

> Have the Levites stand in front of Aaron and his sons and then present them as a wave offering to the LORD. [14] In this way you are to set the Levites apart from the other Israelites, and the Levites will be mine.
> [15] "After you have purified the Levites and presented them as a wave offering, they are to come to do their work at the tent of meeting. [16] They are the Israelites who are to be given wholly to me. I have taken them as my own in place of the firstborn, the first male offspring from every Israelite woman. [17] Every firstborn male in Israel, whether human or animal, is mine. When I struck down all the firstborn in Egypt, I set them apart for myself. [18] And I have taken the Levites in place of all the firstborn sons in Israel. [19] From among all the Israelites, I have given the Levites as gifts to Aaron and his sons to do the work at the tent of meeting on behalf of the Israelites and to make atonement for them so that no plague will strike the Israelites when they go near the sanctuary."

To recap: All the firstborn sons of Israel belong to God. God gives them to the Levites/priests to be part of their family, but God also commands the parents of Israel to redeem their firstborn sons with a specific price.

Even if Jesus was a firstborn and dedicated to the priestly family, He was redeemed; so why does he still get to function as a priest?

THE PRECEDENT is Elkanah and Hannah's firstborn son Samuel, who was dedicated to the Lord and functioned before the Lord as priest and prophet to the people. I Samuel 1:1 establishes that Samuel's father was of the tribe of Ephraim, not Levi. I Samuel 2:11 says "Then Elkanah went home to Ramah, but the boy ministered before the LORD under Eli the priest." This would not be possible unless the Lord allowed it. Remember the rope tied to the ankle of the High Priest when he went in to minister before the Lord in case he was struck dead? If God had been displeased with Samuel serving Him, all Israel would have known about it. Levitical priests outside the line of Aaron ministered to the *people* and performed *sacrifices* (Numbers 4). But only men in the line of Aaron qualified for the job of ministering to the *Lord*, which reinforces Samuel's identity as a priest, since he ministered before the *Lord*.

> **I Samuel 3:19-21** The LORD was with Samuel as he grew up, and he let none of Samuel's words fall to the ground. And all Israel from Dan to Beersheba recognized that Samuel was attested as a prophet of the LORD. The LORD continued to appear at Shiloh, and there he revealed himself to Samuel through his word.

Samuel was well known in Israel to be a priest and a prophet before the Lord and judge of Israel. He anointed Saul as king over Israel and performed the sacrifices for King Saul as only a priest could do. The Lord showed His acceptance of Samuel in this priestly function though he was born outside of the priestly line of Aaron by letting "none of Samuel's words fall to the ground."

Therefore, since Samuel, firstborn of Hannah, could be given to the Lord and become a priest though he was outside the priestly line, Yeshua, firstborn of Mary, can function as a priest, as the firstborn of Israel's family.

Consider this: Because Jesus brought the Kingdom of God to earth the moment He was born, in the Kingdom, Jesus was also the firstborn of many. **Romans 8:29:** "For whom He foreknew, He also predestined to be conformed to the image of His Son, that He might be the firstborn among many brethren." This statement sets Jesus in place as the firstborn in the spirit and the firstborn of Israel.

Jesus also functioned as the sinless man, of whom Adam started out as a prototype. Jesus fulfilled prophecy of being pure and sinless, like the prophetic type of the Passover lamb. Though it was not evident and proven true until after His death, Jesus was the firstborn without sin.

Jesus had the firstborn thing wrapped up: He belonged to God.
- firstborn in physical realm of Mary
- firstborn (only begotten) son of God
- firstborn in the spirit (or Kingdom of God)
- firstborn of Israel as a representative in the Levitical line
- firstborn without sin

Through all of these provisions of the law, Jesus was a priest.

את

HOW A PRIEST IS CONSECRATED

Further evidence of Jesus as our high priest can be found in the way Jesus fulfilled the Torah's description of how a priest was to enter into service. Have you ever wondered: if Jesus was confounding the teachers of the Law in the temple at age 12, why did he wait until he was 30 to begin his ministry?

Here are the requirements according to the Torah for a Levitical priest to begin his duty:

- He must be 30 years old to begin service (Numbers 4:3).
- He must be washed and dedicated (Numbers 8:6-12) a.k.a. be baptized.
- A sacrifice must be made and a hand laid on his head. (Numbers 8:6-12).

Age 30

Numbers 4 cites the age of eligibility of a priest as being between 30 and 50 years old seven times (in verses 3, 23, 30, 35, 39, 43 and 47).

> **Numbers 4:1-3** "Then the LORD spoke to Moses and Aaron, saying: [2] "Take a census of the sons of Kohath from among the children of Levi, by their families, by their fathers' house, [3] from thirty years old and above, even to fifty years old, all who enter the service to do the work in the tabernacle of meeting."

The phrase as underlined above is identical in each of the seven places in Numbers 4. Each place is talking about counting the three different lines of priests, from the family of Kohath, the family of Gershon, and the family of Merari to cover the different jobs associated the priesthood.

Though Numbers 4 seems to solidly establish the age of a priest's eligibility from age 30-50, one time in Numbers 8:23-24, there seems to be an expanded age that started at 25 and ended at 50.

Yeshua had to wait until He was 30 to begin His ministry because that is the age God said a priest had to be in order to be eligible to work.

WASHED AND PURIFIED

The next requirement for priesthood service is for the incoming priest to be washed.

> **Numbers 8:21-22** And the Levites purified themselves and washed their clothes; then Aaron presented them *like* a wave offering before the LORD, and Aaron made atonement for them to cleanse them. [22] After that the Levites went in to do their work in the tabernacle.

BAPTISM

This washing and purification of a new priest must be performed by a priest, but not just any priest, he must be from the line of Aaron. John the Baptist (Yochanan was his real name) baptized Jesus. Does John qualify to purify or baptize a new priest for service?

John's dad was Zacharias.

> **Luke 1:5-6** There was in the days of Herod, the king of Judea, a certain priest named Zacharias, of the division of Abijah. His wife *was* of the daughters of Aaron, and her name *was* Elizabeth. [6] And they were both righteous before God, walking in all the commandments and ordinances of the Lord blameless.

Zacharias had an angelic visitation in his old age in which John's birth was foretold. When Zacharias didn't believe, he was struck dumb until the child's delivery. What was he doing when this prophecy was given? Zacharias was ministering as a priest before the Lord, therefore, according to the list of duties for priests in Numbers 4, Zacharias was in Aaron's line. John's mother, Elizabeth, was also in the priestly line. Therefore John qualified under the Law of Moses as prescribed in Number 8 to baptize new priests for service.

> **Numbers 8:6-7** "Take the Levites from among the children of Israel and cleanse them *ceremonially.* [7] Thus you shall do to them to cleanse them: Sprinkle water of purification on them, and let them shave all their body, and let them wash their clothes, and *so* make themselves clean.

This cleansing and purification had to take place before a new priest could begin his duties. Jesus also, in order to fulfill the Torah, waited until he was 30 years old and was baptized before beginning His ministry.

את

OTHER WAYS JESUS FULFILLS THE TORAH

JESUS AS A SIGN FOR ISRAEL

Jesus did not come to *abolish* the Law/Torah but to *fulfill* it. How does this translate into practice for Christians? First off, don't forget the true purpose and meaning of Torah (a set of instructions to stay on the trail) or that Christians are grafted into Judaism. We were never intended to have to function outside of the Hebraic understanding God set in place in the Torah, yet we Gentiles seem to have set ourselves up in a separate religion. Jesus is the Jewish Messiah and the Jewish hope, not the beginnings of the Christian religion, which is how we have treated Him and the Jews for millennia. Beyond that, we

Christians don't really believe that we are "free from the Law," because we don't live that way. If we *did* believe it, we would commit sins without any thought. Instead somewhere along the line we decided it was Christian to live by the "Top Ten" laws and throw out the others. This practice is normal because we don't understand the Torah or it doesn't seem to apply. This way of thinking can be undone in one statement: Our wrong actions would not be considered "sin," unless there was a foundational standard of righteous and unrighteous which was laid out in the Torah's instruction.

> **Romans 7:7 & 12** What shall we say then? *Is* the law sin? Certainly not! On the contrary, I would not have known sin except through the law. For I would not have known covetousness unless the law had said, "You shall not covet." [12] Therefore the law *is* holy, and the commandment holy and just and good.

We are like the progressives from chapter 1 if we think, "Those old dusty laws have nothing to do with me; I'm past all that." Our culture decided the Law no longer applies. Not only is that idea based in pride (I know better than God) or rebellion (I don't have to follow out-dated laws), but it is accepted without even knowing the full picture of *why* God gave particular instructions. Many of us have rejected God's instructions—His Word—because we don't like or don't understand them; we decided they don't fit with modernity.

I repeat Jesus' own words, "I did not come to destroy the law, but fulfill it" (Matthew 5:17).

There are some laws which are completed and fulfilled in Jesus' life and death, and they have no need of repetition any more, such as blood sacrifice for sin. Paul describes this in Romans 7 like a woman who is unbound from her husband in his death and able to marry another man. Her obligation is fulfilled. There are some ordinances which remain forever, such as celebrating the Feasts of the Lord, the chosen-ness of the Levitical priesthood. Let me be clear, your salvation does not rest on whether you follow these laws or not. Salvation is guaranteed for all who call on Jesus' (Yeshua's) name to cover their sin with His payment. The Jerusalem Council agreed that Gentile believers should also repudiate idolatry to prove that they are following the God of Abraham, Isaac and Jacob (Acts 15). But this verse is presented as if it is the bare minimum.

Instead of arrogantly shouting that "we are no longer under the law," wouldn't it be more productive to acknowledge and receive the ways Jesus fulfilled the law? Moreover, we should be thanking Him for the ways in which He made it easier for us to be righteous before the Living God. In the same way as all things that Jesus changed with His coming, dying and resurrection, life comes down to a heart issue. Let's be a grateful grafted-in-people, rather than an arrogant turn-off for Jewish people and unbelievers.

JESUS, REJECTED OR ACCEPTED BY JEWS?
The Jews living in Jerusalem at the time of Jesus' appearance in history were made up of the 10% of returning-from-exile tribes of Judah and Benjamin and parts of Levi. (This is covered in great detail in *Israel III: Finding Ancient Israel in the Modern Nations*). Many of the Jews who returned home to Israel in the 500-400's BC *did* accept Jesus as the Messiah when He came. Great numbers believed, and many spread all over the ancient world to tell the good news to Jews living abroad, exiles from the northern kingdom of Israel, and Gentiles. Otherwise Christianity would not exist today. It was the *leaders* of Judah and the Levites who rejected Jesus as the long awaited Messiah.

Many Christians today tend to get arrogant and accusatory toward Jews (the dead ones and their modern progeny) who do not accept Jesus when it is quite obvious that He fulfills all the prophecies as Messiah.

But in reality, the Jews are right. Jesus did not fulfill every prophecy record in scripture—there are over 300—at least not with His first coming. Christians have chalked up the unfulfilled parts as being part of His second coming. But at the time of Jesus, a second coming was not a fully realized concept, not until after His death and resurrection when the angles said He would come again (Acts 1:9-11).

Let's take a look at the Jews' reasoning, from the information they had at the time, to help us understand how they could miss Jesus...and keep missing Him century after century.

We will cover the easy part first. According to Rabbi Jamie Cowan,[2] who also used to be a Washington D.C.-based lawyer, the way Jews *keep* missing Jesus is that once a rabbi makes a ruling on a particular issue, it becomes precedent and it is not re-visited. This is similar to how laws function in the United States: once a judge makes a ruling it becomes precedent for other cases. A precedent is almost never challenged much less over turned. So when the rabbis ruled that Yeshua was not the Messiah, it was recorded, and that was that. "Was Yeshua messiah?" is no longer a question to be raised in the Jewish mind.

The second way that the Jews keep missing Jesus is the idea of the two types of messiahs presented in scripture: Messiah, son of Joseph and the Messiah, son of David or Zion.

77

WHAT WERE THE JEWS LOOKING FOR?

With so many prophecies to study, the Jewish leaders (Levites and leading men of Benjamin and Judah) constantly searched for Messiah. This is one of the reasons there were so many rebellions in Judea, besides that their conquerors were so cruel.

Though many common Jews "chose" Jesus as their Messiah, most of the Jewish religious leaders and government disqualified Jesus from being their Messiah because they were looking for the "conquering king." Yeshua had been defeated (crucified). His defeat then, of course, called for them to reject Him as a "false messiah" in order to keep themselves pure for the Holy God, Yahweh. Again, many Jews did not reject Him; that is how we have Christianity.

SON OF DAVID, SON OF JOSEPH

The Torah and Prophets do not teach a second coming of messiah. It teaches two different types of messiahs. Isaiah 53 describes a Messiah son of Joseph (or *Meshiac ben Yosef*), a "suffering servant." Christians understand this one. Jesus was good, served the people, suffered unjustly, and in the end He saved his brothers.

There is an interesting messianic prophecy in Genesis 49:10. It says, "The scepter shall not depart from Judah until Shiloh comes." In itself the thought is prophetic, but beyond that, in Hebrew this verse contains every letter of the Hebrew alphabet except zayin. Zayin is both a letter and a word. It means "weapon." So in the Jewish mind, this prophecy also describes that when Messiah comes, it will be without weapons. This scripture is where the Jewish idea of the suffering servant is derived from.

The second type of messiah, the "conquering king," is found here:

> **Zachariah 14:3-4** Then the LORD will go forth And fight against those nations, As He fights in the day of

battle. And in that day His feet will stand on the Mount of Olives, which faces Jerusalem on the east. And the Mount of Olives shall be split in two, From east to west, *Making* a very large valley; Half of the mountain shall move toward the north And half of it toward the south.

This is a description of the Messiah ben David, (or *Meshiac ben Zyyion*), a picture of the conquering king. As soon as His feet hit the Mount of Olives, it will split, and He will walk down the hill into Jerusalem. At a time when all nations are gathered against Jerusalem, He will step in as the conquering king! With Rome bullying them, the Jews had focused their hope and expectations on this picture of the coming messiah when Yeshua came on the scene!

SOME HEBREW NUMERICAL VALUES

Interestingly, the numerical value of the Hebrew letters that spell Meshiac son of Joseph and the letters that spell Meshiac son of Zion both come out to 156. Obviously the letters in "meshiac ben..." are equal, they are the same letters with a grand total of 424. But the letters in Zion are: tsadek, yod, vav, nun; the letters of Yosef are: yod, vav, samek, peysofit. Between the two names, the only two letters that are the same are vav and yod. (Review the numerical value of letters chart on page 105-106 for details).

A rabbi in Israel who pointed this out said that of all the different numerical possibilities of names and numbers, "the fact that these come out to the same value is rather an anomaly...(It) just shouldn't happen. In the Hebrew language it is quite shocking." He explained that the same number found in the different names of Messiah is a common denominator pointing toward the idea that the two messiah pictures are in fact one in the same, just as Christians see Yeshua.

CONQUERING KING

So on Palm Sunday (the Triumphal Entry) when Yeshua made His way through Jerusalem from the Mount of Olives, people shouted, "Hosannah, Meshiac ben David! Messiah son of Zion!" At that moment Yeshua looked like the picture of the conquering king. In their minds, Jesus didn't exactly have his feet on the Mount of Olives, but He was coming from Bethany which is in the same general direction; He didn't enter through the eastern gate, but He was in Jerusalem; does it have to be exactly to the letter? They were trying to make Yeshua fit their conquering king dream.

Let's jump right into this historical event: The common Jews from all Judea, Samaria, and the Galilee are in Jerusalem for Passover, along with visiting Jews who still lived abroad from the first exile and who were returning to celebrate a the Feast of the Lord. The holy city is bursting at the seams with humanity when they see the miracle worker they've heard rumors about. In the thrill of the moment and not a little anticipation of relief from Roman rule, the people drag out palm branches and wave them in excited worship of the man on the donkey. *And* it is Lamb Selection Day on the Hebrew calendar. "Yes!" they think, "this totally makes sense. This humble man will liberate us from Rome and finally bring us peace! He is the Conquering King Messiah!"

A huge party breaks out in the street, but then Jesus ruins it. He begins crying. He says, "If you had known what will bring you peace…it is not going to be long before your enemies are going to come in and kill you, destroying everything, Not one stone shall be left on another. The way that you're thinking of peace, it is not going to happen that way." (My paraphrase of the event.)

The Jews are pretty sure they found their Conquering King. But Yeshua gets killed. His death quickly changed their paradigm! If they don't shift to the proper understanding of what God is doing in the earth, then they get left behind in the old way of thinking, and are forced to reject Yeshua as the Messiah.

The disciples and many others are able to make that paradigm shift! Acts 1:1-11 describes it. Jesus has risen. The disciples finally understand the servant aspect of messiah by then. So they turn to Jesus and say, "Lord, is it at this time that you will restore the Kingdom of Israel? Now that we have the suffering servant part out of the way, and You've risen from the dead, is now the time for the conquering king, the son of David, part?" Yeshua doesn't say "you don't understand" or "you're crazy." He says, "It is not for you to know the times and epochs of the Father. You've got some other priorities right now."

We've been taught that the disciples are really dull and they still don't get it even after seeing all they've seen, but that's not the case at all. They *did* understand and are now referring to a whole other prophecy. They are saying, "We understand who You are and what You've done, but what about the other part? Is now the time that You are going to establish your literal, physical kingdom and take care of the Romans or anyone else who comes against us?"

Jesus answered them, "Well, it is not 'conquering king' time just yet. Go into Jerusalem and wait for the power of the Holy Spirit." After He said these things, He was lifted up and a cloud received Him out of their sight.

> **Acts 1:10-11** They were looking intently up into the sky as he was going, when suddenly two men dressed in white stood beside them. [11] "Men of Galilee," they said, "why do you stand here looking into the sky? This same Jesus, who has been taken from you into heaven, will come back in the same way you have seen him go into heaven."

Where did He disappear into heaven? It was on the Mount of Olives. Where does this passage say that the Messiah son of David will return to? The Mount of Olives! The angels appeared and said, "Look, guys, the way you saw Him go, is the same way He will come...even on this very spot!" The disciples finally started putting it together. This is how a young Jewish sect, soon to be known as "the Way" which will become Christianity, starts to understand the second coming of Jesus. It is not taught in the Original Covenant. But because the angels showed up and said Yeshua would come back the same way He left, they are starting to get it! Maybe they thought, "We've seen Him fulfill all these other details exactly, so if this is going to be fulfilled too, His feet will have to touch the Mount of Olives and He will come in the eastern gate." So Jesus really did fulfill the details, let's find a few more.

את

JESUS FULFILLS TORAH'S PRICE OF A SERVANT

Did you ever wonder why Judas betrayed Jesus for 30 pieces of silver? Not 50 or 10? The Torah delineates the price of a servant if he was injured to death: 30 pieces of silver was to be paid to the servant's owner. Where did the money paid to Judas come from? The temple treasury. The temple treasury was money given by the people to God. So God paid the price of a servant from his own storehouse. Wow! And thus the law of the Torah in the simple thing such as the price of a servant, Jesus fulfilled.

THE "UNJUST" DEATH OF JESUS

There are two interesting bits of Torah that are not often put together as part of the Torah that Jesus fulfilled.

Deuteronomy 13:1-5 "If there arises among you a prophet or a dreamer of dreams, and he gives you a sign or a wonder, [2] and the sign or the wonder comes to pass, of which he spoke to you, saying, 'Let us go after other gods'—which you have not known—'and let us serve them,' [3] you shall not listen to the words of that prophet or that dreamer of dreams, for the LORD your God is testing you to know whether you love the LORD your God with all your heart and with all your soul. [4] You shall walk after the LORD your God and fear Him, and keep His commandments and obey His voice; you shall serve Him and hold fast to Him. [5] But that prophet or that dreamer of dreams shall be put to death, because he has spoken in order to turn *you* away from the LORD your God, who brought you out of the land of Egypt and redeemed you from the house of bondage, to entice you from the way in which the LORD your God commanded you to walk. So you shall put away the evil from your midst.

Deuteronomy 18:20 [20] But the prophet who presumes to speak a word in My name, which I have not commanded him to speak, or who speaks in the name of other gods, that prophet shall die.'

Based on these two scriptures, God is telling His people, "If a man comes to you proclaiming to be God, even if he does miracles, you are to put him to death, because I am testing your hearts to see if you will hold fast to Me."

So in actuality, God prescribed the death of Jesus in the Torah. God saw that there was going to be a day when He would represent Himself among His people so that He could take their place as punishment for sin, and He told them what they were supposed to do with Him 1500 years ahead of time.[2] He had to die to pay for the sin and God told them that when a man comes and claims to be God, you must kill him. Hmmm! They obeyed (for once!) and it worked out just as God had planned.

את

Did Jesus Miss it?

Jesus became a rabbi. He knew the scriptures (He was the Word, after all!). He was steeped in Jewish tradition. Why didn't He just go ahead and fulfill all the expectations His people had of Him? That way people would know who He was, instead of hiding Himself.

The easy answer to this question is that Jesus was following the plan of the Father to the letter, and two separate visitations had been prescribed before the foundations of the earth. The plan was not supposed to change just because people misunderstood the plan. We are supposed to come into agreement with God's plans, not the other way around.

The deeper question of the heart imbedded in this question is this: it looks like God was trying to trick them, why would God trick His people and not reveal Himself and His plan more clearly? Beyond that, our hearts may ask, "If He hid Himself and tricked them, would He do it again in the end times to me? Am I going to miss it? Am I going to miss Him? What if I don't get it all right?"

Let me set your heart's query to rest: You will miss it! No matter how hard and long you study, even with a spirit of wisdom and revelation, you will not fully be able to lay out every event that will bring about Yeshua's return. But missing it is not the point, just as it wasn't the point the first time He came. The point is shifting our expectations to a new paradigm when it is time. The point is having a relationship of familiarity with Him, so that you recognize His spirit without having to recognize His facial features. A relationship that discards offense when He does something that seems contrary to what you expected is necessary.

If you cultivate relationship with Jesus, you will miss it, but you won't miss *Him*! Just like the first time He came, He made sure that those who sought Him, found Him. He is the same yesterday, today and forever. He will make sure you don't miss Him.

END NOTES

1. I first came across the basics of the Priest and King teaching in a *Jesus in the Torah* Seminar by Doug Hershey given in Richmond, Virginia in 2011. Credit to his industrious research which preceded my own.

2. Cowan, Jamie. 2011. Jewish History Seminar. RIHOP, Richmond Virginia.

5

THE NEW COVENANT

THE NEW COVENANT; THE COVENANT OF JESUS

Oh, did you just think… "finally, we get to our covenant!"? Well, listen to this:

> **Jeremiah 31:31-34** "The time is coming," declares the LORD, "when I will make a new covenant with the house of Israel and with the house of Judah. 32 It will not be like the covenant I made with their forefathers...because they broke my covenant, though I was a husband to them," declares the LORD. 33 "This is the covenant I will make...I will put my law in their minds and write it on their hearts. I will be their God, and they will be my people. 34 No longer will a man teach his neighbor, or a man his brother, saying, 'Know the LORD,' because they will all know me...I will forgive their wickedness and will remember their sins no more."

This New Covenant is definitely made with Israel, and we Gentiles are allowed into their covenant. The New Covenant is fulfillment of all that the Law was. Where the Law exposed sin by giving a list of do's and don'ts, the New Covenant of Jesus gives permanent resolution to that exposed sin.

Old Testament scriptures specifically referring to the New Covenant: Jeremiah 31:31-40; 32:37-42; 50:4-5; Isaiah 59:20-21; 61:8-9; Ezekiel 16:60-63; 34:25-26; 36:24-38; 37:21-28

A trend that I have noticed among Christians is to use the phrase "We are no longer under the law." However where knowledge is lacking, foolishness abounds. Most importantly, the scripture actually says: We are not under the *curse* of the Law (Galatians 3:10-13, emphasis mine). That does not mean the Law is a curse, but we can be free from the curses associated with breaking the Law (as in blessings and curses). There are consequences of sin. I am not saying that those all go away for Christians. But the *curses* associated with breaking the Torah are no longer something we have to worry about when we are covered by the blood of Jesus.

The previous covenants did not disappear; they actually heated up to a new level. Each newer covenant has grown in phases, both in each party's *joy* and the *cost* from the previous one. God did not give the Law just to be spiteful. As we studied before, Torah doesn't even mean "law," it means "a set of instructions to stay on the trail." However for the sake of tradition and cohesion, while we try to untangle some messy thinking, I will refer to Torah as *Law* here.

Every law and principle God gave in the Torah was out of love. Now, 3,500 years later we can see, scientifically, that the outcome of living by these laws brings longevity, or "life more abundant." Hand washing, skin infection care, clean and unclean animals to eat, abstinence before marriage, faithfulness in marriage, keeping the

Sabbath as a day of rest; God even provided instruction for proper handling of waste and corpses. These laws were designed by a loving Father who was explaining to His children how to live well within the world He had created. He knew the laws because He had put them in place. The laws came with blessings and curses for those who obeyed or disobeyed.

PROGRESSION OF THE COVENANT PROGRAM[1]

The Covenant's progression can be followed for ease of recognition by the name of the man involved in "updating it" with God: Adam, Abraham, Moses, David, and Jesus (the New Covenant). In this covenant program that God lays out over centuries, it is important to note, that it was made exclusively with the Jewish people, the seed of Abraham. The only way individuals outside Israel could be part of it was to join themselves to Israel. And while we are still "joining the faithful remnant of Israel" when we become Christians, it is not the same for us in this Era of the Grace of Jesus as it was in the Mosaic Covenant, before Jesus came.

When looking at all the covenants together, a trend emerges. The covenants are building on one another. Could it be that God actually designed this as one big Covenant? As generations pass and our understanding grows, God is imparting more of His ultimate plan to us and asking if we will enter into this new stage of covenant with Him. Dr. Mike Cory[1] of Voice of Judah International Ministries aptly calls this stage-progression of impartation "the Covenant Program."

ADAMIC COVENANT

This covenant began in the Garden where man and God intimately shared life together talking in the cool of the day. Adam represented all mankind in this agreement with God. God gave man two gifts: first, the intimate relationship with Himself that He desired to continue throughout eternity (even knowing ahead of time it would not) and second, authority and dominion to rule over the earth and the animals with Him. Adam and Eve had an obligation for their part of the Covenant too: they could eat of any tree in the garden, except the Tree of the Knowledge of Good and Evil. (Remember, a more accurate translation of this tree's name is Tree of Knowledge of Function and Dysfunction. Up to this time, mankind had only known what it was like to function according to the Creator's plan.)

> **NOAH**
> There was an additional promise/ covenant that occurred in between Adam and Abraham that God made between Him and creation by promising to never completely flood the earth again. Noah was witness to this covenant, and became the new "father of mankind," since the eight people left to repopulate the earth were his family.

When Adam and Eve sinned they forfeited the Covenant plan and benefits for themselves and all of their offspring too. But their disobedience did not change God's desire for deep relationship with man. He had a plan to redeem that intimacy with mankind.

ABRAHAMIC COVENANT

Things on earth had gotten pretty grim with sin, even after the re-boot with the flood, and God searched for a man with whom He could grow a nation and enact his plan of redemption. He found an idol maker named Abram in Ur and invited him into covenant. Abram said yes. The Abrahamic Covenant promised three main things: 1. land, 2. numerous descendants, and 3. blessings on those descendants (Israel), and blessings on the other nations who would bless Israel. Abraham's responsibility was to be circumcised to show himself as a son of the Covenant.

The Abrahamic Covenant was passed down through a particular line of Abraham's offspring, accepting one son and rejecting others in three generations, until Jacob's 12 sons became the 12 tribes of Israel. Abraham's son Isaac was accepted, but Ishmael and others were rejected. Isaac's son Jacob was accepted, but Esau was rejected. I don't know what God saw in these particular men over the others, but they each, Abraham, Isaac and Jacob, had a recorded encounter with God where they reaffirmed the covenant God had made with their father and grandfather, Abraham. This is why He is called the God of Abraham, Isaac, and Jacob, to distinguish Himself from all pagan "gods." Jacob's sons formed the fledgling nation of Israel.

MOSAIC COVENANT

Israel had been made slaves in Egypt and cried out to God to save them. He heard their cry and sent Moses to deliver them. After leading them to freedom, Moses and the people met with God at Mount Sinai where Abraham's Covenant received an update in the covenant program God was enacting. This Mosaic Covenant was a marriage covenant between God and Israel. All the previous promises were still in place, as was Israel's obligation of circumcision. But now there were more obligations and more promises. However these were conditional promises. If Israel would obey God's covenant, they would be blessed; if they disobeyed, curses would befall them. These curses came upon them sometimes as a nation, sometimes as individuals.

During this covenant's enactment at Mount Sinai, the people of Israel began worshipping a golden calf. The Ten Commandments had to be re-etched on new stone tablets, and while God was rewriting, those ten became 613 laws of the covenant between God and Israel. This sounds like a punishment, however, I think it was actually the Lord's mercy. He saw that Israel wasn't prospering and so He spelled out life

91

abundant in a little more detail for them. Israel accepted God's terms of the covenant update and promised to be true to Him and obey all the laws. They received back the land originally promised to Abraham which would make them a light to the nations and draw the nations to God through their example.

The Mosaic Covenant made accommodation for the disobedience God knew would be coming. One of the main curses that Israel would experience if she was not functioning as a proper light to the nations was to be removed from the land of Israel. But God promised that if/when He had to remove them, He would bring them back one day (Jeremiah 30:3) after "seven times" were completed (Leviticus 26: 17-45).

THE DAVIDIC COVENANT

This covenant between David, the second king of Israel, and God had much to do with the coming Messiah through David's family line. David represented all Israel here in that he received a more specific update to the covenant, but also a particular family line of Israel, David's family.

> **II Samuel 7:12-16** "When your days are fulfilled and you rest with your fathers, I will set up your seed after you, who will come from your body, and I will establish his kingdom. He shall build a house for My name, and I will establish the throne of his kingdom forever. I will be his Father, and he shall be My son. If he commits iniquity, I will chasten him with the rod of men and with the blows of the sons of men. But My mercy shall not depart from him, as I took *it* from Saul, whom I removed from before you. And_your house and your kingdom shall be established forever before you. Your throne shall be established forever.""""

This New Covenant involves the highest cost yet. It costs the individual more than just "do not commit adultery." Jesus said if you look with lust upon a woman it is the same as having had the affair with her in your heart. And what about idolatry? The Mosaic Covenant says we shall have no other gods before the one true God. In the New Covenant that costs more than just not bowing before ba'al or molech, God wants us to lay down *any*thing that has more pull or influence on our hearts than He does.

The cost of the New Covenant is our *hearts*, not merely adhering to a list of rules. Following those rules because we want to, honors the way God made the world and helps us to walk in right relationship with the Lord Jesus in the New Covenant.

The benefits of the New Covenant far outweigh the cost: We get to know God, to enter into His presence without fear. We get to partner with Him in bringing His kingdom to earth as is it is heaven. We get to do miracles and participate in healings. We get to know that our names are written in the Lamb's Book of Life, guaranteeing us eternal life with God. Not only that, but God Himself dwells in our hearts through the Holy Spirit now. We get to walk as God's counterpart. How cool is that!? There is no cost too high for this covenant!

This heart-relationship is what God has been after since the Garden. Not only all of the wonderful things listed above, but also, the best thing about the New Covenant is that it is open to all people. Participants don't have to be Jewish, or *act* Jewish to be part of it, as they did in the past. Jesus' Covenant is available to any individual who believes Jesus is the promised Messiah of Israel, the One Who died and rose again to take the punishment for our sinful disobedience, whether we knew we were being disobedient or not.

95

Here is what Jesus Himself says about the New Covenant:

> **Matthew 5:17-24** "Do not think that I came to destroy
> the Law or the Prophets. I did not come to destroy but
> to fulfill. [18] For assuredly, I say to you, till heaven and
> earth pass away, one jot or one tittle will by no means
> pass from the law till all is fulfilled. [19] Whoever
> therefore breaks one of the least of these
> commandments, and teaches men so, shall be called
> least in the kingdom of heaven; but whoever does and
> teaches *them,* he shall be called great in the kingdom
> of heaven. [20] For I say to you, that unless your
> righteousness exceeds *the righteousness* of the scribes
> and Pharisees, you will by no means enter the
> kingdom of heaven.
> [21] "You have heard that it was said to those of old,
> 'You shall not murder, and whoever murders will be
> in danger of the judgment.' [22] But I say to you that
> whoever is angry with his brother without a cause
> shall be in danger of the judgment. And whoever says
> to his brother, 'Raca!' shall be in danger of the
> council. But whoever says, 'You fool!' shall be in
> danger of hell fire. [23] Therefore if you bring your gift
> to the altar, and there remember that your brother has
> something against you, [24] leave your gift there before
> the altar, and go your way. First be reconciled to your
> brother, and then come and offer your gift.

FOUNDATIONAL PROMISES AND PROVISIONS OF THE NEW COVENANT[1]

These are the main promises and provisions under this updated
covenant manifested in Jesus. Cory's[1] following list shows them all
together with where they are described.

1. It is an unconditional covenant of grace, resting on the "I will" of
God. (Ephesians 1:7.)

2. It is an everlasting covenant (Abrahamic: Genesis 17:7; Jesus/New: Ezekiel 16:60; 37:26).

3. In an identity exchange we receive a renewed heart and mind (Ezekiel 11:19; 36:26; Romans 10:16).

4. It grants forgiveness of sin with our request (Acts 5:31; 26:18).

5. It gives us the promised indwelling of the Holy Spirit: Receive power and teaching by and know the will of God by the Holy Spirit in our hearts. (Luke 12:12; John 14:26; Acts 1:8; Acts 10:45 specifically includes Gentiles; Acts 15:28 wisdom.)

6. When Israel is in the land she will be blessed materially (Jeremiah 31:1-38).

7. There will be a rebuilt physical temple/sanctuary in Jerusalem (Daniel 9:27; II Thessalonians 2:3-4). Beyond that, we are now the temple of the Holy Spirit (I Corinthians 6:19-20).

8. War shall cease and peace will reign on the earth. (Isaiah 65:17-25; Micah 4:3; Isaiah 2:4)

In the New Covenant, through Yeshua, we experience the total fulfillment, *and integration*, of all the previous covenants God made with Israel.

IT IS ALL ABOUT A PROMISE[1]

It started in the Garden with Adam (Genesis 3:15). The promise was further developed and given to Abraham and then to all Abraham's descendants through Moses. Even though they were given guidelines to stay on the trail toward the promise, Israel's receiving of the promise did not depend on their performance. They were measured by their *faith in the promise* and the Promise Giver. The promise was partially fulfilled in Messiah's first coming and every aspect will come about with Messiah's second coming.

All of those original principles are still in place and we will do well to follow them. The difference now is that when we disobey the law (sin), if we have entered into the New Covenant with Jesus being the payment for our disobedience, we are given grace, if we ask for forgiveness. Jesus paid our debt for us. Jesus was sent to earth, lived a blameless (sin free) life and then gave His life as the payment for all the sins of man.

> The Church is part of a much bigger plan than what it had realized. The promises and blessings inherited by the Church (through being grafted in) are connected to the promises which existed long before the birth of the Church, many of which have yet to be fulfilled.[3] (p.18)

BLOOD SACRIFICES OF THE COVENANTS

Sin requires death as payment. God requires blood.

Romans 6:23a For the wages of sin is death…

The payment for sin is still required. It is the way God set up His universe. It is still true in the New Covenant. It doesn't get cancelled out. But that is not the end of the verse! (or the end of God's thought.)

> **Romans 6:23** For the wages of sin is death, but the gift of God is eternal life.

God provided an answer to the wages: Himself. In the same way that gravity still existed after we discovered the principles of flight, those flight principles must be invoked in order to trump the law of gravity. We must accept Jesus paying for our sin in order for His sacrifice to cover *our* sin.

The blameless lambs-and-goats-provision God put into the Abrahamic covenant were only placeholders for Jesus, the one who would be *the* Blameless Lamb sacrificed in payment for sin. They were a picture of Who was to come from the very beginning. Remember the 10-generation prophecy of Genesis 5 from the names of Adam through Noah (chapter 3)? Jesus was always God's plan.

Since He has now come and paid the price, the sacrifice of white fuzzy lambs is no longer necessary. We are not "abolishing" sacrifices, or any part of the covenant; Jesus finished it for us. Jesus Himself tells us He fulfilled the covenantal law in Matthew 5:17. Rabbi Shaul (Paul) later wrote about this gift of Jesus coming in the flesh to fulfill the law of the covenant's death/blood mandate. Jesus brought peace between mankind and God's law.

> **Matthew 5:17** "Do not think that I came to destroy the Law or the Prophets. I did not come to destroy but to fulfill.

> **Ephesians 2:15** having abolished in His flesh the enmity, *that is,* the law of commandments *contained* in ordinances, so as to create in Himself one new man *from* the two, *thus* making peace.

On the surface and without context these verses sound contradictory, but they actually say the same thing. To us, the law acted as or seemed like an enemy, because it pointed out our sin which keeps us from relationship with God. Jesus came and fulfilled the blood mandate of payment, and yet never broke the Covenant Himself; therefore He made peace for us and relationship available with God.

This all happened just as God said it would because He is a faithful God.

To Keep Torah or Not to Keep Torah?

That is the question, isn't it? Congregations, even ones that get the "Israel thing" go round and round on this issue using words like "completed" "abolished" "done away with" "made null and void" "fulfilled" and "everlasting" to make their arguments for and against Christians and Messianic Jews keeping Torah law.

It is illogical to claim on one hand that the Law is "done away with" and on the other hand that the "Word of God is living and powerful, sharper than any two-edged sword" (Hebrews 4:12). I don't think any Christian really believes that God's Word is null and void.

What we have failed to grasp is that Torah was never *mandatory* in the first place. We, in our Pharisaical pride, have twisted this whole covenant relationship back to front. We've taken it from relationship into legalism when we say "thou shalt keep Torah." The Torah was a new constitution for the nation of Israel freed from Egypt.[4] And it was based on Temple or Tabernacle worship, neither of which exist anymore since the second Diaspora in 70 AD. If the Torah is required for anyone, logically, it is required for everyone. And not in part but in whole. Which is impossible because of the missing temple.

Keeping Torah law, as the Holy Spirit brings conviction into your heart is based on relationship and brings about holiness. But if you abide by some hokey holier-than-thou self determination to "not eat pork because the Torah calls it unclean" you are probably not going to be successful. And if you do happen to not give in in this area, some other area of your life, such as pride, will be out of control. Your self-determination will never be determined enough without the grace of God. However, if you are prompted by the Holy Spirit to give up pork as a "life-long fast," you can do it, and it becomes a private way to honor and worship the Lord, a special thing between the two of you. And if you end up at a BBQ where pork is being served, you simply decline politely, "no thank you. I'm just having a cheese sandwich with my salad today." There is no need to give the cook an entire explanation on why pork is not kosher while you're holding up the line. Please. Let the Holy Spirit convict whom He will, and don't worry about anyone else. And remember, when the Holy Spirit brings conviction about any particular behavior, and it happens to be in the Torah, it is your "yes" of obedience that brings further holiness to your relationship, not that the law is being followed. And He always acts in our best interest, not to be mean or withhold anything from us. So sh'ma (listen and obey) for His conviction as an act of love between the two of you.

GRACE

Perhaps the best way to conclude this discussion is to clarify this word *grace* that we throw around as if it is a synonym of mercy. Usually I hear grace "defined as 'undeserved merit,' and that may be the Greek definition, but it was translated from spoken Hebrew and the original concept of grace is the empowerment of God to overcome sin. Grace doesn't simply *cover* sin (that is mercy), grace prevents it in the first place."[4(para 12)]

So when we talk about the era of grace we live in under Jesus' blood, we should start understanding it, not as He cleans up the messes we make with sin in our lives because we are fallen men, but rather, His grace provides the empowerment to overcome sin[4] and sin patterns in our lives forever. Jesus' grace prevents the sin; His mercy removes the guilt after we sin. That is what living in the era of grace really means!

Should we still endeavor to study and understand the Torah then? Absolutely. The Torah is the Word of God and never loses its power. However, we should not presume that everyone will be convicted of the same things in the same formula order as anyone else. If followed as the Holy Spirit directs in *your* life, the Torah's instruction will bring you into holiness and life abundant. It will bring about the "set apart for a specific purpose" that God has for *you*. We cannot force anyone into holiness.[4] Sin can still destroy a person. Believer or not. So a wise man will study the "instruction to stay on the trail" that his Maker provided for him.[4]

END NOTES

1. Mike Cory's teachings can be found at www.voiceofjudah.com. Covenant program information retrieved May 14, 2013 from http://voiceofjudah.com/index.php?option=com_content&view=articl e&id=12&Itemid=33

2. Information on the exilarchs of Israel and a dated listed can be found at http://www.peerage.org/genealogy/exilarch.htm

3. Cory, Mike. 2012. Israel, the Church and the Kingdom. Seminar Notes published by Voice of Judah International, Atlanta, GA. p.18.

4. Pearce, Ted. 2014. Facebook status update retrieved April 30, 2014 from https://www.facebook.com/#!/ted.pearce.18?fref=ts

COVENANT PROGRAM FLOW CHART

Note: Each new updated Covenant requires more from each party.

Adamic Covenant:
Adam: no eating from tree
God: gives authority to rule & Intimacy with God

Abrahamic Covenant:
Abraham: Circumcision

God: gives land, a son & blessed descendants

Mosaic Covenant:
Moses & Israel: Previous plus circumcision for all & 613 Laws of Torah
God: Bless & prosper a whole nation

Davidic Covenant:
David: all previous plus heart worship

God: David's Seed ruling Israel's throne forever

Millennial Kingdom Covenant:
One New Man: previous plus nations come worship God in Jerusalem

God: No war or crying. Brings peace, martyrs rule for 1000 years with Yeshua; rain on earth.

New Covenant (Jesus):
Israel & Gentiles: rend our hearts and motives

God: forgive sin, bless Israel in Land, writes His law on hearts

6

THE TALLIT

The tallit is also called a prayer shawl. The word *tallit* in Hebrew refers to "a tent or covering." It is worn all the time today among devout Jewish men (and some women), and the tradition finds its origins in the commands of the Torah.

> **Numbers 15: 37-39** The LORD said to Moses, "Speak to the Israelites and say to them: 'Throughout the generations to come you are to make tassels on the corners of your garments, with a blue cord on each tassel. You will have these tassels to look at and so you will remember all the commands of the LORD, that you may obey them and not prostitute yourselves by chasing after the lusts of your own hearts and eyes.'"

But what does that mean? What does it look like? And most importantly, how does it function? The "corner of your garment" is pretty self-explanatory (until you come to the modern era where our clothes don't generally have corners. We will come back to that and just study the original for now.) In Hebrew, the corner is called *knof.* The tassels are called *tzitzit* (pronounced "seat-seat"). It is a fringe. Fringe in the ancient days was tied in certain ways to show who a person was, mostly for the servants of kings and other noble people. God is so practical; He values things we can see, touch, feel, smell and taste to teach us about Him. Therefore, He designed a way for the Hebrew people to always have before them a designation of to whom they belong. A Gentile could identify their roles in life and who they served by looking at their garments.[1] So God's command served a practical purpose: to remind His people that they belonged to Him and to point them out as His to others.

The tzitzit[3] are attached to the knof with knots, and are tied with eight cords (seven white cords and one blue cord) in a series of five knots with the blue cord wrapped between the knots. The blue cord is called *shamash* in Hebrew.[2] It translates to English as "caretaker, servant or custodian." The word *shamash* is found other places in Jewish culture and language too. It is the word used for the taller light in the middle of the hanukkiah (candelabra), which is used to light the other candles at Hanukkah. *Shamash* refers to the central stem of the menorah as well. The blue shamash in the tzitzit is wrapped in succession 7, 8, 11, and 13 times between the five knots. It may be hard to imagine if you've not seen one. In explanation: all the cords are knotted, then the blue cord is wrapped around the seven white cords 7 times, then they are all knotted again, then the blue cord is wrapped 8 times to the next knot...and so on.

HOW DOES THE TALLIT FUNCTION AS A REMINDER?

To begin to answer, like any good Jew, I'll answer the question with another question: What is a religious Jew reminded of when he sees the five knots of the tzitzit? Or, what does the number 5 represent to the Hebrew mind? The five books of the Torah.

Beyond the most basic reminder of the Covenant of Moses in the five knots, there is a "secret" numbering hidden within the tzitzit. As you may have studied before each Hebrew letter is also used in the Hebrew numbering system. The chart below is the same as the one in chapter two, but the numerical value has been added in column two and makes the letter-number value designation for you.

Alef	1	א	A vowel sounds
Bet	2	בּ/ב	B/V
Gimmel	3	ג	G
Dalet	4	ד	D
Hey	5	ה	H
Vav	6	ו	V or vowel sound
Zayin	7	ז	Z
Chet	8	ח	Ch/guttural
Tet	9	ט	T
Yod	10	י	Y/I vowel sounds
Kof (Kofsofit)	20 (500)	ך כ/כּ	K or ch
Lamed	30	ל	L

Mem (Memsofit)	40 (600)	ם מ	M, soft m
Nun (Nunsofit)	50 (700)	ן נ	N, soft n
Samech	60	ס	S
Ayin	70	ע	Vowel sounds, other
Pey Peysofit	80 (800)	ף פ/ﬔ	P/f
Tsadi Tsadisofit	90 (900)	ץ צ	Ts/Z
Kuf	100	ק	Q/K
Resh	200	ר	R
Shen	300	שׂ/שׁ	S/Sh
Tav	400	ת	T

The Hebrew letters used to spell *tzitzit* are tav, yod, tsadek, yod, tsadek. The value of these letters as seen in the chart above are tav=400, yod=10 and tsadek=90. When the value of each letter is added together (400+10+90+10+90), the value of the word tzitzit equals 600. When also adding the number of knots (5) and the number of cords (8), this provides a grand total of 613. Does that sound familiar? It is the exact number of laws recorded in the Torah for the Jews as their foundation for following the Torah.

BUT WAIT, THERE'S MORE!

The blue cord, *shamash* or the caretaker, in the way in which it is wrapped designates the very name of God. Rabbi Abraham Millgram[2] describes it like this:

> (I)n making the fringes one winds the long thread around the other threads between the 5 knots 7, 8, 11, and 13 times respectively. The first three numbers

108

equal 26, which is the numerical value of the Tetragrammaton. The remaining number equals the numerical value of the word *ehad* (meaning "one")-- the last word in the opening verse of the Shema. The fringes of the *tallit* thus not only remind the Jew of the 613 divine commandments, but also underscore the central doctrine of Judaism, that the Lord is one.

Tetragrammaton refers to the unspeakable name of God, spelled in Hebrew: yod, hey, vav, hey. Therefore the wrapping of the caretaker spells out numerically "Yahweh One." This idea of God being One is the foundation of the very center pillar of Judaism: God is one. It comes from their daily beginning and ending prayer, "Hear, O Israel: the Lord our God, the Lord is one (God)" (Deuteronomy 6:4).

This foundation scripture prayer is called the *Shma*. The Hebrew word *shma* means "to hear." But within shma is also the idea of not just listening, but "to hear *and obey*." Now speak the words aloud: Shma. Shamash. They sound so similar. Because this shma—hear and obey—concept also sounds like shamash, could there also be a connection in the Jewish mind when seeing the blue shamash with the shma command to hear and obey?

So as the Jew runs his fingers through the tassels on the corner of his garment as he is working in the fields, sitting at the table, working at the bank or praying, he has a kinetic reminder of the Torah in the knots that interrupt the wrapped "caretaker" cord that tells him, the Lord his God is one God and is the caretaker of the Jews. He also has a symbol in the name tzitzit of the 613 laws he is supposed to keep, and he is always to be wearing this tallit, so it is a constant reminder. It reminds him of who he is, his identity and his function in the world.

BLOSSOMS PRODUCE FRUIT

The word *tzitzit* (the fringe) is derived from the root word *tzit* which means blossom. So not only does the Jew remember the Laws of God from the tassels, their very name means blossom, doubled. And what does a blossom produce? In the Hebrew way of thinking: what is a blossom's function? A blossom produces fruit, which is exactly what the Jew wearing his tzitzit will be doing in life when He is following the commands of his God!

TABERNACLE is another reference to the tallit in scripture. The wearer would bring the tallit up over his head and as he bowed in prayer, the tallit would surround him and hem him in like a tent or tabernacle, blocking out all distractions.

GARMENTS WITH NO CORNERS

Most clothes starting in the Middle Ages[4] until now have not had corners on which to attach the tzitzit. But that has not kept devout Jews from following the commands of God. They designed a sleeveless poncho-like garment, with square corners, which they put on over their head and it hangs, front and back, about waist length. On those corners they tie the fringy strings of the tzitzit, trimmed to about an 8- to 12-inch length. Currently, Jewish men wear this style of tallit (called *tallit katan*, or small tallit) either under or over their everyday garments. When worn underneath, the tzitzit hang out, to show their devotion to God, and be the reminder God intended for the tzitzit to be.

תא

HAVE WE OVERLOOKED THE TALLIT IN OUR BIBLE?

ELIJAH AND ELISHA

Remember in II Kings 2 when Elijah is about to be taken to heaven and Elisha is sticking closer than glue, wanting his anointing, his cloak, his mantle? Not only that, Elisha wanted double! Elijah is taken to heaven in a whirlwind and Elisha sees it happen. Elijah's cloak fell away from him as he went.

110

II Kings 2:13-15 Elisha then picked up Elijah's cloak that had fallen from him and went back and stood on the bank of the Jordan. He took the cloak that had fallen from Elijah and struck the water with it. "Where now is the LORD, the God of Elijah?" he asked. When he struck the water, it divided to the right and to the left, and he crossed over. The company of the prophets from Jericho, who were watching, said, "The spirit of Elijah is resting on Elisha." And they went to meet him and bowed to the ground before him.

So what was this cloak with the miraculous powers that Elisha received? It was Elijah's tallit! It had the same power, yet doubled, just as Elisha requested. Interestingly, the Bible records exactly double the number of miracles of Elisha (16) as it does of Elijah (8).[5]

SAMUEL THE PROPHET AND KING SAUL

Samuel was a true prophet of the Lord and would have been wearing the tallit in accordance with God's command. King Saul also would have been wearing the tallit, as his position over Israel demanded. Let's go back to the story in I Samuel 15 when Samuel comes to King Saul after the Amalakite king, Agag was spared in disobedience to God.

Samuel has had enough of Saul's excuses for disobedience. (I Samuel 15: 17-23, 27-29, 34-35)

> [17] Samuel said, "Although you were once small in your own eyes, did you not become the head of the tribes of Israel? The LORD anointed you king over Israel. [18]And he sent you on a mission, saying, 'Go and completely destroy those wicked people, the Amalekites; wage war against them until you have wiped them out.' [19] Why did you not obey the LORD? Why did you pounce on the plunder and do evil in the eyes of the LORD?"

> [20] "But I did obey the LORD," Saul said. "I went on the mission the LORD assigned me. I completely destroyed the Amalekites and brought back Agag their king. [21] The soldiers took sheep and cattle from the plunder, the best of what was devoted to God, in order to sacrifice them to the LORD your God at Gilgal." [22] But Samuel replied:
> "Does the LORD delight in burnt offerings and sacrifices as much as in obeying the LORD? To obey is better than sacrifice, and to heed is better than the fat of rams. [23]For rebellion is like the sin of divination, and arrogance like the evil of idolatry. Because you have rejected the word of the LORD, he has rejected you as king."
> [27] As Samuel turned to leave, <u>Saul caught hold of the hem of his robe, and it tore</u>. [28] Samuel said to him, "The LORD has torn the kingdom of Israel from you today and has given it to one of your neighbors—to one better than you.

So looking at this story and paying special attention to verse 27, "Saul caught hold of the hem of his (Samuel's) robe, and it tore," what would have been located at the "hem of his robe" that would have torn? It was the tzitzit that Saul tore from Samuel's tallit! It wasn't just an object lesson that popped into the prophet's mind when he saw the tassel separated from his tallit. It was a prophetic event that showed Samuel what God was doing to Saul, and Samuel just lets Saul in on it when he says, "The Lord has torn the kingdom of Israel from you today…"

SAUL AND DAVID

The tallit and tzitzit come up again later in Saul's life. Remember when Saul is chasing David in the wilderness and has to go into a cave to relieve himself.

> **I Samuel 24:4-7** David crept up unnoticed and cut off a corner of Saul's robe. [5]Afterward, David was

conscience-stricken for having cut off a corner of his robe. [6] He said to his men, "The LORD forbid that I should do such a thing to my master, the LORD's anointed, or lay my hand on him; for he is the anointed of the LORD." [7] With these words David sharply rebuked his men and did not allow them to attack Saul. And Saul left the cave and went his way.

The "corner" of Saul's robe is the *knof*. This is the place where the tzitzit are attached. David did not slice a random piece of hem that was closest to him. The knof and the tzitzit are what David removed from Saul's garment!

Then David came out of the cave after Saul and shouted to get his attention. When Saul turned around, David fell to the earth bowing and said, (24:10-11)

> This day you have seen with your own eyes how the LORD delivered you into my hands in the cave. Some urged me to kill you, but I spared you; I said, 'I will not lay my hand on my lord, because he is the LORD's anointed.' [11] See, my father, look at this piece of your robe in my hand! I cut off the corner of your robe but did not kill you.

Can you imagine King Saul's mind working overtime right then? Picture David standing in the distance against the background of the rocky hills of Ein Gedi; he's holding the knof with the strings of the tzitzit with their distinct shape fluttering in the breeze as he waves them over his head.

When was the last time that Saul saw a tzitzit detached from a tallit like this? The day Saul disobeyed God and the kingdom was ripped from him!

The sight must have taken him right back to that moment, because Saul has an immediate change of attitude that seems more significant than just his "normal" wild mood swings. I think Saul felt the kind and gentle hand of the Lord's correction and rebuke, in the way that only the Lord can do. Even in front of a crowd of people, no one else there, including David, would have understood what God was reminding Saul of: "That the kingdom of Israel did not belong to Saul." Listen to the change in Saul.

> **I Samuel 24:16-21** When David finished saying this, Saul asked, "Is that your voice, David my son?" And he wept aloud. [17]"You are more righteous than I," he said. "You have treated me well, but I have treated you badly. [18] You have just now told me about the good you did to me; the LORD delivered me into your hands, but you did not kill me. [19] When a man finds his enemy, does he let him get away unharmed? May the LORD reward you well for the way you treated me today. [20] I know that you will surely be king and that the kingdom of Israel will be established in your hands. [21] Now swear to me by the LORD that you will not kill off my descendants or wipe out my name from my father's family."

It is these last statements, "I know that you will surely be king" and "swear to me...you will not kill off my descendants" where Saul shows that it is finalized in his mind that the kingship no longer belongs to him. He has been humbled by the Lord (at least for the time being). He knows with certainty that David will be king in his place, not Jonathan his son, and Saul calls on the integrity that David just displayed in not killing Saul when he could have, to get him to promise that *when* he is king, he will not kill Saul's family.

FROM DAVID'S POINT OF VIEW

Now, if we switch our point of view to David's and look at this story, we see a whole different scenario. David was getting just a little antsy in his waiting to be king and his men were <u>not</u> encouraging him to wait on God's perfect timing! Plus the current king was trying to murder him. So David just snuck up and decided to show off a little of his prowess as a mighty warrior. Maybe he thought, "I'll just put the fear of God in him." But soon God was pricking David's heart (24:5-6).

> [5] Afterward, David was conscience-stricken for having cut off a corner of his robe. [6] He said to his men, "The LORD forbid that I should do such a thing to my master, the LORD's anointed, or lay my hand on him; for he is the anointed of the LORD."

What do you suppose David was thinking? He saw Saul's royal tzitzit (a declaration of who Saul was and to whom he belonged, in addition to being the symbol of God's law) in his own hand and David's conscious brought shame upon him. He had separated his king from the reminder of the commands of God! Saul was already having trouble keeping the commands of God and had been separated from the voice of the Lord through Samuel. Could David be so cruel as to separate God's anointed from even the *reminder* of the 613 Laws? Who knows if Saul might one day repent and be restored to God.

So David, in genuine sorrow, called out and bowed low to Saul who was God's anointed. Was there ever a more clear moment of distinction in character between these first two kings of Israel? Saul in his murderous rage is confronted by a man after God's own heart— who doesn't even know he is confronting Saul—and causes a melting heart to bring about repentance and acceptance of God's future plan for Israel. All from a "slight of hand" God plays with a tzitzit!

JESUS

It was commanded for Jews to make for themselves a tallit and wear it as a reminder, and Jesus obeyed every law in the Torah, therefore Jesus made and wore a tallit.

"Wings" was a Jewish nickname for tzitzit, probably from the way they fluttered slightly behind when a person walked. One of the prophecies about the coming messiah from Malachi 4:2a is "But to you who fear My name the Sun of Righteousness shall arise with healing in His wings." Now most of the great prophets could heal; that didn't take much faith at all. But healing in his wings was a whole other level of anointing.

While Jesus was ministering there was a woman with a 12 year long issue of blood flow.

> **Mark 5: 27-29 NLT** She had heard about Jesus, so she came up behind him through the crowd and touched his robe. [28] For she thought to herself, "If I can just touch his robe, I will be healed." [29] Immediately the bleeding stopped, and she could feel in her body that she had been healed of her terrible condition.

When she approached Jesus in the crowd and grabbed hold of "the hem of his garment" (as the Matthew 9:20 version of this story goes), it was the tzitzit she grabbed hold of. Jesus felt the healing power go out of Him, and told her that her faith had healed her. With as many prophets as could heal, I don't think it was this woman's faith in Jesus' ability to heal her that made the difference in her situation. Because of the way she intentionally touched the wings of Jesus' garment she demonstrated that she believed Jesus was the Messiah. I think it was her faith in *who* Jesus was, that He was the Messiah, which healed her body.

PAUL

Paul refers to himself as a "tentmaker." I had always pictured him making homes for people like a camping tent or a Bedouin tent. In all likelihood, with his background as a rabbi, Paul was not working with canvas, poles and tent pegs. Paul would have been creating tallits and tying the knots of the tzitzit with precision on the knof for the Jews abroad to purchase while he was making his missionary rounds. The word *tent* is a reference often used for the tallit.

Judaism (before and after Jesus) was a very evangelistic religion for several centuries between 150 BC and 300 AD.[6] New converts and the Jews living abroad either from the first Diaspora, as missionaries, or for economic reasons would all need tallits to wear. The Jews wouldn't have had such a "kosher" source available for their new additions to the family who would be bar mitzvah-ing and needing one of their own. Tallits could wear out through use. Replacements would be needed. Then this rabbi, who studied under the renowned Gamaliel, swept through town teaching Torah on the Sabbath and introducing a new interpretation of the Torah, and had with him new tallits he constructed himself. What Jewish family living outside the community of Jews who returned from the exile wouldn't buy one? Even if the Jews had followed the law to "make for yourselves" tallits, it would be nice to have a special occasion prayer shawl. Therefore keeping Paul in business would have been as simple as getting the materials to make the tallit-tents.

את

DID JESUS HAVE A TATTOO?

John describes Jesus returning with "King of Kings and Lord of Lords" written on his thigh. Some Greek-thinking people (especially the modern, tattoo-crazed society) have decided that these words have been tattooed onto His thigh. There are a couple of problems with that line of thinking.

1. Jews are forbidden to have their skin tattooed, and Jesus doesn't break the commands of the Torah
2. It is missing a functional Hebrew perspective

Here is the scripture where the idea originated.

> **Revelation 19:11-16** I saw heaven standing open and there before me was a white horse, whose rider is called Faithful and True. With justice he judges and wages war. His eyes are like blazing fire, and on his head are many crowns. He has a name written on him that no one knows but he himself. He is dressed in a robe dipped in blood, and his name is the Word of God. The armies of heaven were following him, riding on white horses and dressed in fine linen, white and clean. Coming out of his mouth is a sharp sword with which to strike down the nations. "He will rule them with an iron scepter." He treads the winepress of the fury of the wrath of God Almighty. On his robe and on his thigh he has this name written: KING OF KINGS AND LORD OF LORDS.

By adding our new knowledge of the meaning of the tallit and its cords, knots, and tassels, we can picture Jesus wearing His tallit while He is riding His white horse. Where do the knof and the tassels which spell the name of God fall? Right on His thigh, just as they do on every Jewish man who sits, whether it be astride a horse, in a chair, or on the floor. The name of God is written in every properly tied tallit, and also Jesus' tallit as it falls on His thigh at the end of the age. He doesn't have a tattoo, He is wearing His tallit.

THE FLAG OF ISRAEL[7]

In 1897, in Basel, Switzerland at the first Zionist Congress, the Jews were meeting together to form what would become 50 years later the new State of Israel. In the planning stages for the meeting they discussed what flag their new nation would congregate under. I can imagine all these statesmen doodling little symbols and choosing colors in the margins of their papers. Now keep in mind, this was not a spiritual prophetic movement to reform God's nation of Israel. These were secular Jews for the most part. But it doesn't make any difference to the Lord's purposes. David Wolfson, a distinguished Zionist leader who in 1904 succeeded Herzl as president of the World Zionist Organization, said,

> "At the behest of our leader Herzl, I came to Basel to make preparations for the Zionist Congress to assure its success and avoid any opening for detractors. Among the many problems that occupied me then was one which contained something of the essence of the Jewish problem. What flag would we hang in the Congress hall? Then the idea struck me: We have a flag! It is blue and white. The tallit in which we wrap ourselves when we pray. That is our symbol. Let us take this tallit from the bag and unroll it before the eyes of Israel and the eyes of all the nations. So I ordered a blue and white flag with the shield of David painted upon it. And that is how our national flag that flew over the congress hall came into being. And no one expressed any surprise or asked when or how it came from."

It made complete sense to all who saw it! It didn't matter where people came from, which country, whether they were rich or poor. They recognized their national symbol, because God was rallying people under his Torah. Moses and the commands of God are the unifying thing of Israel and the Jews. God reformed the new State of Israel under the banner of the covenant that they had always worn as part of their identity and the reminder of their belonging. They are proclaiming to the world, whether they recognize what they are saying or not, "We are living under the covenant we have with the God of Abraham, Isaac and Jacob. We are Israel." Their prophetic destiny is being fulfilled!

END NOTES

1. Hanefesh. (n.d.) The holy deed of wearing the tallit. Retrieved February 28, 2013 from http://www.hanefesh.com/edu/Tzitzit_Shawl_Prayer.htm

2. Millgram, Abraham Rabbi d.1998. (n.d.) The tallit: Spiritual significance. My Jewish Learning.com. Retrieved Feb 28, 2013 from http://www.myjewishlearning.com/practices/Ritual/Prayer/Ritual_Gar b/Tallit_Prayer_Shawl_/Spiritual_Significance.shtml

3. Ginsburg, Harav Yitchak. (n.d.) The Tzitzit. Gal Einai Institute. Extended explanation was retrieved March 4, 2013 from http://www.inner.org/613-mitzvot/tzitzit.php

4. Jacobs, Louise Rabbi. (n.d.) Tallit,(the prayer shawl). My Jewish Lerning.com. Retrieved March 29, 2013 from http://www.myjewishlearning.com/practices/Ritual/Prayer/Ritual_Gar b/Tallit_Prayer_Shawl_.shtml

5. Hunt Michael. 2001. Elijah and Elisha: The great prophets of God. Agape Bible Study. Retrieved March 4, 2013 from http://www.agapebiblestudy.com/charts/Miracles%20of%20Elijah%2 0and%20Elisha.htm

6. Jews as evangelists from Jamie Cowen's Jewish History Seminar notes. Recorded Spring 2011, Richmond, Virginia, RIHOP. The reasons were more for building political clout outside Judea than gaining religious followers, but still the story of God made it outside the borders of Israel.

7. The story and quote of the Israeli flag being of the origin of a tallit is from "Teachings on the Torah" Seminar notes, Doug Hershey, Spring 2011, Richmond, VA. RIHOP.

7

THE FEASTS OF THE LORD

On Day Four, in the beginning, God instituted the times and seasons. They are called *moedim* in Hebrew. *Moedim* (spelled mem, vav, ayin, dalet, yod, memsofit) can be broken into smaller parts, the "im" is the Hebrew way of making a word plural. "Moed" (mem, vav, ayin, dalet) means "to appointed."

> **Genesis 1:14-19** Then God said, "Let there be lights in the firmament of the heavens to divide the day from the night; and let them be for signs and seasons, and for days and years; ¹⁵ and let them be for lights in the firmament of the heavens to give light on the earth"; and it was so. ¹⁶ Then God made two great lights: the greater light to rule the day, and the lesser light to rule the night. *He made* the stars also. ¹⁷ God set them in the firmament of the heavens to give light on the earth, ¹⁸ and to rule over the day and over the night, and to divide the light from the darkness. And <u>God saw that *it was* good</u>. ¹⁹ So the evening and the morning were the fourth day.

A literal or "mechanical" translation of verse 14 from Hebrew to English by Jeff Benner[1] says:

> "and-he-will-Say Elohim [Powers] will-be-Exist Luminary-s in-Sheet the-Sky to-make-Separate Between the-day and-Between the-night and-they-did-Exist to-Sign-s and-to-Appointed-s and-to-Day-s and-Year-s"

You could think of *moedim* as "an appointment" or "set time" or a "time that is set." God set the appointments with man to set aside a time to draw near to each other. *Moedim* is used many times throughout scripture and translated several different ways[2]: 150 times the word *moed* is translated "congregation;" 23 times as "feast;" 13 times as "season;" 12 times each as "appointed" and "time;" 4 times the word *moed* is translated "assembly."

A pair of examples of *moed* translations from Genesis:

> **Genesis 18:14** Is anything too hard for the LORD? At the appointed time I will return to you, according to the time of life, and Sarah shall have a son."

> **Genesis 21:2** For Sarah conceived and bore Abraham a son in his old age, at the set time of which God had spoken to him.

God based the Hebrew calendar on the cycle of the sun, moon and stars (which God made) so that man could observe and follow the passage of time (which God also made). God exists outside of time; He invented it for our good, a way for us to organize events and life. And to wax a bit philosophical here, the need for time is the need for man to mark the way toward something and from something. Specifically toward the End. Both the end of a man's life on earth, and the end of life as we know it. It is a way to keep track and have order. Some *moedim* occur again and again in an anticipated way on the calendar, several *moedim* are one-time events. The keeping of Shabbat is a weekly *moed*. The new moon feast is a monthly *moed*. Passover is an annual *moed*. Messiah's birth is a unique one-time *moed*.

Specific events have hurled us at an ever increasing pace toward the end of days. The Flood, the giving of Torah, the coming of Messiah, the founding of the New World, Israel's rebirth and the return of the Jews, and still to come are the Great Tribulation, the second coming of Messiah, the Millennial Reign and Satan being cast into the Lake of Fire. Each of these major events has changed, and will change, the way life is done forever. Minor recent events along the way also include the Protestant Reformation, the invention of the printing press, the Industrial Revolution, the rise of democracy and civil rights, the rise and fall of communism, the dawn of the Age of Information. God put in place times and seasons. These include both the seasons of society and the weather seasons.

> **Genesis 8:22** While the earth remains, seedtime and harvest, cold and heat, winter and summer, and day and night shall not cease.

Society follows the pattern God set in place—a calendar—where seasons are recurring. Daniel adds to our understanding that God is controlling seasons of life and time itself when he records:

> **Daniel 2:21** And He changes the times and the seasons; He removes kings and raises up kings; He gives wisdom to the wise And knowledge to those who have understanding.

God also loves us and doesn't want us to miss the changing of a season, so as usual, God does it in a big way. God broadcasts in the sky when a *major* seasonal shift is coming.

It is fascinating that the two most significant events in history, the first and second coming of Messiah, will have signs among the sun, moon and stars, which God created to show man that events on earth are taking place. The wise men from the east saw the star at Messiah's birth (Matthew 2:1-2) and scripture records that the moon will turn to blood and the sun and stars will become diminished (by one-third) at Messiah's return (Isaiah 13:10, 34:4, Matthew 24:29 & Joel 2:30-31).

> ### TRIES TO CHANGE TIME ITSELF
>
> Later in Daniel's record he mentions an anti-Messiah who will "...speak *pompous* words against the Most High, Shall persecute the saints of the Most High, And shall intend to change times and law. Then *the saints* shall be given into his hand For a time and times and half a time." (Daniel 7:25). Again Satan tries to usurp what belongs to God, in this instance the ability to control times and seasons.

God knew at the beginning when these two major world-changing events would occur, so He set in place markers in the calendar as well as the signs in the heavens. He was working overtime so that mankind would not miss them.

The first and second coming of Messiah occur to bring about restored relationship—that Eden-like relationship—between God and man. So there are events that function both as actual events of redemption, and also as symbols of the greater coming redemption. As they happen, God tells Moses to write them down, along with instructions on how to celebrate and commemorate them. God calls them "Feasts of the Lord." The Jewish people experienced the original events and observe them as holidays, as they were instructed, "throughout their generations" (Leviticus 23:21-41). Leviticus 23:31 is even more specific saying that the generations of Hebrews shall celebrate these feasts no matter where they live. "(I)t shall be a statute forever throughout your generations in all your dwellings." So whether living in Israel or scattered among the empires or nations, the Jewish people are commanded to celebrate the Feasts of the Lord.

God calls these Feasts (or remembrances) "holy convocations" (Leviticus 23:2). We talked about what holy (*kodash*) means already: set aside for a specific purpose. Convocation (*mikrah*) means "a rehearsal" (Strong's # 4744). So God is referring to these Feasts of the Lord as "a set time, reserved in advance, for a specific purpose of rehearsing." Rehearsing can be thought of as a time of "re-hearing" what God is doing.

> **Leviticus 23:1-3 NKJV** And the LORD spoke to Moses, saying, "Speak to the children of Israel, and say to them: 'The feasts of the LORD, which you shall proclaim to be holy convocations, these are My feasts. Six days shall work be done, but the seventh day is a Sabbath of solemn rest, a holy convocation. You shall do no work on it; it is the Sabbath of the LORD in all your dwellings.

We will search out later what these Feasts of the Lord are "rehearsals" for!

תא

THE FEASTS OF THE LORD

SHABBAT

From the scripture above, the very first Feast of the Lord that God describes is the weekly Sabbath rest. It is also known as *Shabbat*, or *Shabbes*. The word *Shabbat* does not mean Saturday. It is any prescribed "rest day." There is a weekly Shabbat that falls on Saturdays, the seventh day of the week. There are also feast days that are Shabbats. Shabbats are *moedim* or days of prescribed rest before the Lord. Specific days He wants to meet with His people. During a week-long feast, usually the first and last days are Shabbats, days of rest. The people are to do no work on those days.

It is the varying definitions of "work" that cause the controversies and "fences" around the holiday so as not to break the law on these Shabbat days. The scripture only says "shall do no work" (see Leviticus 23:1-3 above).

The phrase "in all your dwellings" as the Lord describes the Shabbat rest means just what you think it does: Wherever the Jewish people will dwell, whether inside the land of Israel or in exile by force, or living abroad by choice, they are to observe the Sabbath and keep it holy.

The Shabbat is a sign between God and His people. It was modeled by the Creator God in the first week as recorded in Genesis 1. The Shabbat is in itself an appointed time, and just like all the other *moedim,* it speaks prophetically. The Shabbat speaks to the Jewish people and also to believing Gentiles of a future event: the ultimate rest we will have in Messiah at the end of this Age.

> **Hebrew 4: 9-11** There remains therefore a rest for the people of God. For he who has entered His rest has himself also ceased from his works as God *did* from His. Let us therefore be diligent to enter that rest, lest anyone fall according to the same example of disobedience.

THERE IS ALSO A SHABBAT YEAR. It is called the *shemitah.* Leviticus 25 describes it. The Jewish people are to count off six years and then during the seventh year, they are to allow their fields to rest. No sowing!

> **Leviticus 25:3-5** Six years you shall sow your field, and six years you shall prune your vineyard, and

gather its fruit; but in the seventh year there shall be a Sabbath of solemn rest for the land, a Sabbath to the LORD. You shall neither sow your field nor prune your vineyard. What grows of its own accord of your harvest you shall not reap, nor gather the grapes of your untended vine, for it is a year of rest for the land.

JUBILEE. Every seventh *shemitah* year, there is an extra celebration. Leviticus 25:8-55 describes that every seventh Shabbat year (every 49 years) the year following the Shabbat year is a Year of Jubilee; it is the 50th year. (two back-to-back Shabbat years every 50 years.) The Year of Jubilee is the Shabbat Year of Shabbat years! The whole year is dedicated to the Lord. It is when families are put back together and land is redeemed by original owners, valuables that have been sold are returned (Leviticus 25:10). Slaves are set free, debts are forgiven. The Jubilee is a once or perhaps twice in a lifetime celebration.

In fact, because this concept is always ahead in their minds, the Jewish people are actually *leasing* their land or valuables or indentured servitude according to the number of years remaining until the Jubilee for land, or until the shemitah year for all the others. Only a house located inside city walls can be sold forever.

PROVISIONS FOR THE SEVENTH AND EIGHTH YEARS. So if they are anything like me, I'm sure the Israelites were wondering, "so if we are not planting or harvesting, or preserving food for the next (eighth) year, how are we going eat until we harvest the plantings of the 8th year in the ninth year?" God took care of that before they had time to ask:

> **Leviticus 25:21-22** Then I will command my blessing on you in the sixth year, and it will bring forth produce enough for three years. And you shall sow in the eighth year, and eat old produce until the ninth year…

So God was going to produce a bumper crop every sixth year, and the blessing would already be in the cupboard/barn etc. before they had to act on (or NOT act, in this case) the sabbath year's rest.

All of this so far, and the Shabbat is just one *moedim*! The Feasts of the Lord are described in Leviticus 23 and occur in lumps together, a group of them in the Spring each year and a group of them in the Fall each year. So we will study them in the order in which they appear both on the calendar and in scripture.

תא

THE SPRING FEASTS OF THE LORD

In the order of their occurrence on the annual calendar the spring feasts are Passover, Unleavened Bread, First Fruits, and the Feast of Weeks. (These are their names in English; the Hebrew name will be discussed as we discuss each holy convocation day).

PASSOVER

In Hebrew Passover is called *Pesach*. This holy convocation was instituted as a one-day feast to occur annually on *Aviv* (now called *Nissan*) 14. Passover is its own holiday, but it also occurs on the day before the next holiday (Feast of Unleavened Bread). Passover commemorates the passing of the Angel of Death over the homes marked with the blood of the lamb according to God's instructions through Moses. The instructions for duplicating the actual meal are specific and given here:

> **Exodus 12:6-10** Now you shall keep it (the lamb) until the fourteenth day of the same month. Then the whole assembly of the congregation of Israel shall kill

it at twilight. [7] And they shall take *some* of the blood and put *it* on the two doorposts and on the lintel of the houses where they eat it. [8] Then they shall eat the flesh on that night; roasted in fire, with unleavened bread *and* with bitter *herbs* they shall eat it. [9] Do not eat it raw, nor boiled at all with water, but roasted in fire— its head with its legs and its entrails. [10] You shall let none of it remain until morning, and what remains of it until morning you shall burn with fire. [11] And thus you shall eat it: *with* a belt on your waist, your sandals on your feet, and your staff in your hand. So you shall eat it in haste. It *is* the LORD's Passover.

Today the meal's great significance remains. It is a bond among Jews reminding them of their identity as the chosen Children of the Most High. It is carried out similarly among Jewish communities and families from modern Israel and in the US, to ancient Babylon, to Soviet Russia, to feudal Europe in the Middle Ages, to Spain, Britain and Germany in the 1400's, to Persia, Algeria, Arabia, Tunisia and Ethiopia in the 1800's. For 3,000 years this Passover meal and celebration of songs and order of prayers has barely changed. Participants taste the bitter herbs and dip the unleavened bread; they consume the sacrificial lamb and cry out, "next year in Jerusalem!"

THE FEAST OF UNLEAVENED BREAD
This Feast of the Lord lasts seven days beginning as Passover day ends and ending seven days later on *Aviv/Nissan* 21. However, since unleavened bread is such a major part of Passover, and all the leaven has already been taken out of the house by that day, I think Passover day should bring the count to eight days. (That is my opinion as an intense bread-lover!) During the Feast of Unleavened Bread, the first and last days of the feast are the Shabbat no-work days, the ones in between are still part of the feast. They require a sacrifice to be made and no leaven is to be consumed or brought into the house, but they

are regular work days. All the children of Israel are to eat only unleavened bread for seven days.

The unleavened bread serves as a reminder of the days after their rescue from Egypt when all they had was unleavened bread (Exodus 13:3-10).

> **Exodus 13:8-9** And you shall tell your son in that day saying, 'This is done because of what the Lord did for me when I came up out of Egypt. It shall be a sign to you on your hand and as a memorial between your eyes, that the Lord's law may be in your mouth; for with a strong hand the Lord has brought you out of Egypt. You shall therefore keep this ordinance in its season from year to year.

FIRST FRUITS (*BIKKURIM*)

First Fruits is called *Bikkurim* in Hebrew. The one-day Feast of the Lord First Fruits occurs annually on the first "first day of the week" after Passover. Since Hebrew days of the week don't have names, "the first day of the week" means the day after the weekly Shabbat, which Jews call the seventh day. So the day after that, or the first day of the week, we would call Sunday. It comes about *during* the Feast of Unleavened Bread as the first Sunday after Passover.

The Jewish people are to celebrate *Bikkurim* by bringing "a sheaf the first fruits of your harvest to the priest. He shall wave the sheaf before the Lord to be accepted on your behalf" (Leviticus 23:10b-11a). Then there are other sacrifices made: a one-year old unblemished lamb, plus fine flour, oil and wine. It is also prescribed:

> **Leviticus 23:14** You shall eat neither bread nor parched grain nor fresh grain until the same day that you have brought an offering to your God; it shall be a

statute forever throughout your generations in all your dwelling.

Usually, as the first fruit bud appears on trees or the first grain comes up, the farmers tie a red string or thread around the branch to distinguish it from the others as they begin to produce too, so that they will know which fruit belongs to the Lord. The *Bikkurim* kicks off the harvest season for grains which lasts about six to eight weeks; they are days of gladness in Israel. There are seven species that the Lord has especially blessed to grow in Israel and sustain God's people there, and each of the seven species is brought to the Lord at the Temple as an offering on *Bikkurim*: grapes, figs, olives, pomegranates, wheat, barley, and dates. Each species has its own harvest season beginning with barley in late spring and ending with pomegranates in late fall.

SHAVUOT OR THE FEAST OF WEEKS

This one-day *moedim*'s timing is based on when *Bikkurim*/First Fruits occurs. It is a Shabbat-no-work holiday. The Israelites were to count off seven Shabbats, and on the next day, which would be the 50th day (7 days x 7 weeks= 49 days +1 day = 50) after First Fruits, then celebrate *Shavuot* or the Feast of Weeks. The days in between are called Omer, or the counting of the Omer. According to Leviticus 23:15-22, the Israelites were to bake two loaves of bread with leaven and fine flour and offer them to the Lord as a wave offering, along with seven unblemished, one-year-old lambs, one young bull, and two rams as a burnt offering. They are also to give their regular grain offering and drink offering which will provide "a sweet aroma to the LORD." After those offerings, a sacrifice is made of one kid goat for a sin offering and two year-old male lambs as a peace offering. The priest is to wave this along with the bread before the Lord.

The Feast of Weeks or Shavuot brings the last of the grains harvest seasons. The barley harvest is in and the wheat is being harvested during this time. There are additional instructions for land owners during Shavuot: when harvesting your crops, leave the corners of your field for the poor and the stranger.

The Jewish people celebrate this as the day the Torah was given on Mount Sinai, even though it is not specifically given in the Bible as the reason for celebrating Shavuot.

Currently, one of the ways Shavuot's day off is celebrated in the land of Israel currently is to eat dairy and cheese products, cheesecake and cheese blintzes. This man-made tradition was picked up to start celebrating the giving of the Torah. In their thinking, before Torah, it made no difference what they ate, but after the giving of the Torah, they were to eat kosher.

Also it is tradition to study the Torah all night on this night! Both men and women participate.

> In Jerusalem, tens of thousands of people finish off the nighttime study session by walking to the Western Wall before dawn and joining the sunrise minyan there. This practice began in 1967. One week before Shavuot of that year, the Israeli army recaptured the Old City in the Six-Day War, and on Shavuot day, the army opened the Western Wall to visitors. Over 200,000 Jews came to see and pray at the site that had been off-limits to them since 1948. The custom of walking to the Western Wall on Shavuot has continued every year since.[5]

SPRING FEASTS GROUPING. All these Spring Feasts are grouped together from the Passover which is linked to the Feast of Unleavened Bread by the continued eating of unleavened bread and its proximity on the calendar of running into each other, to the First Fruits/*Bikkurim* which falls during Unleavened Bread. Then, the Counting of the Omer which starts at First Fruits and leads to *Shavuot*/Feast of Weeks. These are the *moedim* which the Lord has prescribed. A time of meeting with Him!

את

THE FALL FEASTS OF THE LORD

The Fall Feasts are usually referenced in their Hebrew name (as opposed to the English translation as has happened to the Spring Feasts). In order of their occurrence they are as follows: *Teshuva* (season of repentance), *Rosh Chodesh* (head of the month), *Yom Teruah* (The day of shouting/trumpets) a.k.a. *Rosh HaShanah*, *Yom Kippur* (Day of Atonement), *Sukkot* (Feast of Tabernacles/Booths), *Simchat Torah/Shemini Atzeret* (Assembly of the eighth day/ "Rejoice in the Torah").

TESHUVA

Teshuva is a 40-day season of repentance that occurs throughout the group of Fall Feasts, or "high holy days." Teshuva begins at sundown on Elul 1, as the new month is beginning when the new moon has been sighted and confirmed and ends on *Yom Kippur*. This is a time of lengthy introspection as the High Holy Days approach.

Teshuva occurred in the history of Israel after the golden calf incident when Moses ascended Mount Sinai the second time. He went to receive the Torah for 40 days (a second 40-day period of absence). While Moses went to plead with God, the people lived in wonder of whether God would forgive their sin, so according to Jewish tradition, they were in constant repentance during the events of Exodus 33 and 34.

During this 40-day period, the shofar is sounded every morning to "awaken people's hearts to repentance," in remembrance of this fearful time during Israel's history. The Jewish sage Rambam, Moses Maimonides (1135-1204 AD), said the shofar's sound carries this urgent message: *"Arise from your slumber, you who are asleep; wake up from your deep sleep, you who are fast asleep; search your deeds, repent, remember your Creator."*[3] The trumpet is not blown on Sabbaths, nor on the last couple of days of the month during Teshuva.

YOM TERUAH

Yom Teruah goes by several names: *Rosh Hashanah* (head of the year) or the Day of Trumpets or the Day of Shouting, or the Hidden Day, also *Yom ha Din* (the Day of Judgment). It is a single day though. It occurs annually on Tishrei 1 [which is also a *Rosh Chodesh* (head of the month), like Teshuva]. It is interesting because the Hebrews of old didn't exactly know which day this convocation would begin each year. The new moon had to be sighted and confirmed by a witness before the trumpet was blown to announce the commencement of the new month (Tishrei) which was also the beginning of a new year. There are a couple of days of darkness as the cycle of the moon transitions each month. This waiting to sight the new moon occurred every month, and was referred to with an idiom in Hebrew which means: *the day and hour which no one knows.* However this is the only holy convocation which occurs on "the day and hour which no one knows." Because no one knew exactly which day this would happen (one of three possible days) it is sometimes called the "Hidden Day."

Yom Teruah is the day the last trumpet is sounded from *Teshuva.* (It is the 31st day of *Teshuva's* 40 days.) It is when the judgment begins. Jewish rabbis teach that on *Yom Teruah* God will begin His judgment of men, finishing up on Yom Kippur.

Yom Teruah's trumpets and shouting comes from

> **Numbers 29:1** On the first day of the seventh month
> hold a sacred assembly (holy convocation) and do no
> regular work. It is a day for you to sound the trumpets.

The word *Teruah* (Strong's #8643) means "alarm, signal, shout (as if
splitting the ears) or blast of war, alarm or joy."[6]

Jewish historic tradition says that *Tishrei* 1 is the day that "the first
man and woman also repented their sin, introducing the concept and
opportunities of teshuvah return into the human experience."[4] The
word *teshuvah* literally means "return."[12] When God judged that
Adam and Eve had sinned, they repented, and this portion of the
Torah is read in synagogues worldwide on Yom Teruah.

Traditionally Yom Teruah is the day that the books of judgment are
opened in heaven. According to Michael Rodkinson's translation of
the Babylonian Talmud,

> Three books are opened on New Year's Day: one for
> the utterly wicked, one for the wholly good, and one
> for the average class of people. The wholly righteous
> are at once inscribed, (in the Book of Life) and life is
> decreed for them; the entirely wicked are at once
> inscribed, and destruction destined for them; the
> average class are held in the balance from New Year's
> Day till the Day of Atonement; if they prove
> themselves worthy they are inscribed for life, if not
> they are inscribed for destruction…From the passage
> [Psalms, lxix. 29]: "Let them be blotted out of the
> book of the living, and they shall not be written down
> with the righteous."[7]

At this Yom Teruah judgment is when men are found to be righteous,
wicked, or in between. If classified as "in between," their final

judgment is withheld for 10 days. Ten days, presumably, to repent and get themselves made right with God.

YOM KIPPUR

Ten days after *Yom Teruah/Rosh Hashanah/* Day of Trumpets it is time for the next Feast of the Lord, *Yom Kippur*. It is the holiest day of the year, also known as the Day of Atonement. *Yom Kippur* occurs on the 40th and final day of Teshuva, it falls annually on *Tishrei* 10. It is the final day of judgment and is a solemn day of fasting in all Israel. It is definitely categorized as a no-work Shabbat.

Originally, *Yom Kippur* is the day Moses re-entered the camp at Mount Sinai with the new Ten Commandments, bringing with him a "national atonement" for their sin of worshiping the golden calf.

God set in place as recorded in Leviticus 23:26-32 that *Yom Kippur* is a day of complete fasting from all food and water for all Israel. *Yom Kippur* is the day that the High Priest of Israel enters the Holy of Holies to meet with God face to face. That was when they still had a Holy of Holies to enter (Tabernacle and Temple Eras). The priest would wear holy white linen garments (Leviticus 16:4) and make three sacrifices and sprinkle the blood on the mercy seat (between the wings of the two angels on the lid of the Ark of the Covenant). He would come face to face with God. Then he returned to pray over the people face to face. It was the only day of the year when the most holy name of God was spoken: the tetragrammaton, yod, hey, vav, hey.

THE TWO GOATS OF YOM KIPPUR. The entire chapter of Leviticus 16 is devoted to the rituals and sacrifices required on the Day of Atonement. It includes the Jewish tradition/commandment of two goats. The two are assigned their duties by casting lots. One goat is marked "for the Lord;" it is sacrificed as a sin offering and its blood is sprinkled on the mercy seat. The other goat is marked "for Azazel." (Azazel is a name for Satan from the Book of Enoch). The second goat receives the sin of the people spoken over it, thus becoming cursed. A person is designated to lead it into the wilderness and push it off a cliff to its death.[9]

Usually the Jewish people wear all white clothing (to remind themselves that they have been marked as righteous) on Yom Kippur and at sunset on Yom Kippur, after a full day of fasting food and water, they eat a meal together to break the fast at synagogue. This last service at the synagogue is called *Neilah* meaning "locked" in Hebrew. It is when the three books of judgment are closed or "locked" whether for righteousness or wickedness. There is no longer an intermediate category of judgment.[9]

SUKKOT–FEAST OF TABERNACLES

This modeim is also known as the Feast of Booths because the Israelites were commanded to build booths and live in them for a week. In Biblical Hebrew it is referred to as the "Feast of the Ingathering"[8] (Exodus 23:16). This Feast of the Lord lasts for 7 full days and falls annually on Tishrei 15th -22nd just five days after Yom Kippur. The first and last days of this feast are no-work Shabbats.

This Feast of the Lord, Sukkot, is a rehearsal and remembrance of the time Israel spent in the wilderness learning a new way of life with the God of Abraham, Isaac and Jacob as their sole provider. It is a remembrance of the first years that they tabernacle'd with God, and God's desire to live with Israel even in the desert wilderness.

Sukkot also celebrates the final fruits and vegetables harvest. The first rains of the year in the land of Israel usually fall just as this feast is ending each year.

The specifications on the *moedim*:

> **Leviticus 23:40-43 NKJV** And you shall take for yourselves on the first day the fruit of beautiful trees, branches of palm trees, the boughs of leafy trees, and willows of the brook; and you shall rejoice before the LORD your God for seven days. [41] You shall keep it as a feast to the LORD for seven days in the year. *It shall be* a statute forever in your generations. You shall celebrate it in the seventh month. [42] You shall dwell in booths for seven days. All who are native Israelites shall dwell in booths, [43] that your generations may know that I made the children of Israel dwell in booths when I brought them out of the land of Egypt: I *am* the LORD your God.'"

BOOTHS. Therefore, based on this scripture, they build themselves *sukkahs*/booths or tent-like structures and eat dinner and have people over for sukkah parties on different nights all week. Sometimes people sleep outside in their sukkahs. Most people run electricity out to their sukkah for lights, music and fans. You might imagine what this is like inside a large city. Sukkahs are erected on sidewalks, roofs, balconies, and in postage-stamp sized backyards all over Jerusalem. Even restaurants get involved and build sukkahs for their patrons to eat inside or outside during Sukkot. It is a huge, loud celebration and family time, especially after the solemnity of Yom Kippur.

THE FOUR SPECIES OF SUKKOT.[11] According to Leviticus 23:40 the Jewish people are to take these four species of the harvest and rejoice before the Lord with them: 1. fruit of the beautiful tree 2. palm branches 3. leafy tree boughs and 4. willow boughs. So they do. The Etrog (or citron fruit) is used as the fruit of the beautiful tree, and the other three branches don't really need additional explanation, though a myrtle tree branch is used for the leafy tree bough. The three tree species are bound together and referred to as "the palm" since it is the largest species of the grouping (called *lulav* in Hebrew). They recite a blessing and wave the four species north, south, east, west, up and down to symbolize that God is all around us. This waving is also done during the religious service during prayer.

Sukkot or Feast of Tabernacles is the only feast mentioned as being celebrated in the following way: **Zechariah 14:16** "Then the survivors from all the nations that have attacked Jerusalem will go up year after year to worship the King, the Lord Almighty, and to celebrate the Feast of Tabernacles."

The Feast of Tabernacles will endure perpetually!

SHEMINI ATZERET (ASSEMBLY OF THE 8TH DAY)
SIMCHAT TORAH—"REJOICING IN TORAH"

Just as the seventh and final day of Sukkot comes around, another day of celebration is tacked onto the end! *Simchat Torah* falls annually as the final 8th day of the seven-day Feast of Sukkot, on *Tishrei* 22. It is the day that the annual reading of the torah portions is completed. The concept behind this 8th day is that "everyone is preparing to go home (from the seven-day feast)...(b)ut God has enjoyed His people so much that He *begs* them to stay an additional day."[10]

Shemini Atzeret is considered The Last Great Day.

DO CHRISTIANS HAVE TO KEEP THE FEASTS?

"Why wouldn't you want to?" is a better question.

The "Christian holidays" we have now, Christmas and Easter, were established by pagans. Wouldn't it be better to celebrate God's holidays by entering into His appointed times and draw near to Him as we remember His awesome works and also look forward to what He will do in the future?

The only things *required* of Gentile Christians are laid out by Paul/Rabbi Sha'ul

> **Acts 15:19-20** It is my judgment, therefore, that we should not make it difficult for the Gentiles who are turning to God. [20] Instead we should write to them, telling them to abstain from food polluted by idols, from sexual immorality, from the meat of strangled animals and from blood.

All four of these items are actually one thing in the Jewish mind: Believers are to forsake idolatry (each item is part of the worship of idols as practiced by Gentiles in this era). But there is more available than just what is *required* of Believers! The Feasts of the Lord are times (*moedim*) that God has said He will be found by us if we search for Him.

It is my opinion that the Church at large which refuses to celebrate the Feasts of the Lord is suffering because of judgments we have made against the Jewish people for being "bound by their own traditions of man." Now we are stuck in the same predicament: we are bound by our own traditions of Christmas and Easter. We justify our celebrations by saying that the pagan holidays have been "redeemed" by Jesus' blood, so it is okay to celebrate them. And sure, that's fine. But is that *all* you want? It is not the fullness that God has made available! God has set up times and seasons full of imagery that didn't need redemption. He made these appointments for us. They are still in place. Some of them have double meanings already fulfilled within history while some of them have prophetic messages about still future events.

It's a party, for Yeshua's sake! (pun intended!) Come on out and celebrate, don't miss an appointment with God for lack of knowledge. Study, find out what the Feasts mean, and celebrate what God has done and will do! (The next chapter will discuss these prophetic aspects of the Feasts of the Lord).

END NOTES

1. Benner, Jeff. 2007. A Mechanical Translation of the Book of Genesis: The Hebrew Text Literally Translated Word for Word. Virtual Book Worm Publishing. This book can be ordered online and will change the way you read scripture. ISBN-13: 978-1602640337

2. Info on *moedim*'s number of occurrences retrieved June 5, 2013 from http://www.mashiyach.com/chagim/moedim.htm. (C) 2005 Mashiyach website, Author Baruch Ben Daniel.

3. Cory, Michael. 2012. Israel, the Church and the Kingdom Seminar Notes. Voice of Judah International Ministries, Atlanta, Georgia. pg 105. His quote taken from Orthodox Union—Enhancing Jewish Life. "Elul, A time to Reflect—Arise from your Slumber." www.ou.org/chagim/elul/arise.html

4. *Tishrei* 1 historical significance retrieved June 5, 2013 from http://www.chabad.org/calendar/view/day_cdo/aid/150487/jewish/Doves-3rd-Mission.htm

5. Quote about Jerusalem taken from http://en.wikipedia.org/wiki/Shavuot under section 3.5 on modern traditions. Retrieved June 14, 2013.

6. Cory, Michael. 2012. Israel, the Church and the Kingdom Seminar Notes. Voice of Judah International Ministries, Atlanta, Georgia. Pg 108.

7. Babylonian Talmud, Book 2: Tracts Erubin, Shekalim, Rosh Hashana, translated by Michael L. Rodkinson, [1918], at sacred-texts.com. Chapter one: New Year. Retrieved June 14, 2013 from http://www.sacred-texts.com/jud/t02/ros03.htm page 26 as listed in text.

8. Feast of Tabernacles called Feast of Ingathering in Exodus 23:16: http://www.mechon-mamre.org/p/pt/pt0223.htm#16 retrieved June 14, 2013.

9. Description of the two goats: Cory, Michael. 2012. Israel, the Church and the Kingdom Seminar Notes. Voice of Judah International Ministries, Atlanta, Georgia. Pg 115.

10. Quote from Cory, Michael. 2012. Israel, the Church and the Kingdom Seminar Notes. Voice of Judah International Ministries, Atlanta, Georgia. Pg 121.

11. Info on the 4 species retrieved June 19, 2013 from http://www.jewfaq.org/holiday5.htm. There is a lot more on this holiday's current observances listed on this webpage.

12. Pelaia, Ariela. (n.d.) What is Teshuvah? Judaism from About.com. Retrieved January 16, 2014 from http://judaism.about.com/od/judaismbasics/g/teshuvah.htm

8

REHEARSALS:
THE FEASTS OF THE LORD

REHEARSALS

With all the amazing celebrations surrounding the Feasts of the Lord, I would like to point out something even more spectacular about what God is doing when placing these *moedim* or holy convocations into the culture of the Jewish people. Remember that a holy convocation is a time set apart for a specific purpose of *rehearsing*. What is being rehearsed? Is it the stories of the miraculous past being retold and remembered among generations of Jewish people? Yes, but there's more. (With God there is always more!)

THE SPRING FEASTS of the Lord correspond (to the exact day and time!) in order on the calendar with the last days of Messiah's first coming. Most Christians have had Passover explained to them. (If not, there is a clear and basic explanation in my book *Israel Basics: What Every Christian Should Know*). Passover, both the meal and the traditions, from choosing a perfect lamb, to the time of the sacrifice, from hand-washing to being examined by leaders from all of Israel's factions of leadership correspond to final-week (a.k.a. passion week in Christian circles) of Yeshua. The choosing of a lamb, examining it and killing it for the sins of the people the way God set it up was a rehearsal for when Yeshua would come as the Lamb of God, and Israel would choose Him, examine Him, and kill Him for the sins of the people. The blood of a perfect lamb, once and for all! Down to the very minute, Yeshua fulfilled not only the Torah's descriptions of this feast, but also many of the traditions that made their way into the Jewish culture over the centuries!

But did you connect that the day Yeshua rose from the dead was also a prescribed Jewish rehearsal day/Feast of the Lord day? Yeshua rose from the dead on the first "first day of the week" after Passover. Of course it was a Sunday, because First Fruits/*Bikkurim* always falls on a Sunday. Christians call it Resurrection Sunday, but Jesus was fulfilling the First Fruits Feast of the Lord by becoming the first among many who would rise from the dead in the Kingdom of God in the last days! Talk about first fruits!

Not only that, the counting of the Omer began that *Bikkurim* day. During this same 50-day counting period Yeshua was on earth for 40 days in His heavenly body popping into sealed rooms and talking with people on the Emmaus Road and disappearing. When Yeshua ascended to heaven from the Mount of Olives, He told his disciple friends to wait for the Holy Spirit to come. They waited...for 10 days in the upper room. Then the Holy Spirit descended in tongues of fire on the 120 gathered in waiting on *Shavuot* (the Feast of Weeks). In Christian circles we call it "Pentecost" because of the number 50 involved (40 days + 10 days from Jesus' death). So on the first *Shavuot* God gave the Torah to Israel on Mount Sinai, and they remembered and rehearsed for 1500 years, and another *Shavuot* God gave the Jewish people and the Gentiles His Holy Spirit on Mount Zion! Both are a manifestation of the spirit of God. Remember the scripture from John 1:1? "In the beginning was the Word, and the Word was with God and the Word was God." The Torah is the Word of God (Yeshua) sent to guide the people in what is right. The Holy Spirit is God sent to dwell within us. It is all God, and all different persons, which lands us smack in the middle of the Trinity.

The Spring Feasts of the Lord have been rehearsals lasting 1,500 years for the first coming of Messiah!

Passover= Jesus' death
First Fruits= Jesus' resurrection
Shavuot=Giving the gift of the Holy Spirit

את

THE FALL FEASTS

Now we come to the Fall Feasts. Hold onto your hats! They are rehearsals for the Second Coming of Messiah! In the same way that the Spring Feasts were fulfilled in order and on the exact day of the Feasts of the Lord, the Fall Feasts will be fulfilled.

I know you've been told "no one knows the day or hour" of the Lord's return, but consider this a moment: what if it was Yeshua making a play on words! There is a Jewish idiom for *Yom Teruah/Rosh Hashanah* which is an <u>actual day</u> called "the day and hour that no one knows." The Jewish people knew the 2-3 day window of time when the day could begin, but not the exact moment when the month began, and therefore when the Feast, began. Thus it came to be associated with the nickname "the day and hour which no one knows." I'm sure it sounds a little catchier in Hebrew.

Matthew 24:3 is where the disciples ask the question about the Lord's return. From verse 29-31 Yeshua talks about his return at the *conclusion* of end time events. Matthew 24:36 is where the phrase "no man knows the day or hour" comes from. The disciples talking with Yeshua would have had no trouble associating His phraseology with the idiom and therefore the appointed day: *Rosh Chodesh* and *Yom Teruah*. Yeshua did not mean that his return will occur on some *random* day and hour that no one but the Father knows, but that He would come back on *Yom Teruah*!

That just flew in the face of the Church's interpretation of Hebrew scripture going back nearly 1900 years! Misunderstanding and missing pieces are what happened when the Church decided to separate herself from the "habitat" that God originally intended Christianity to thrive in. God intended that the Gentiles be part of fulfilled, Yeshua/Jesus-embracing Judaism. This separation will be covered in chapter 9 on the split between the Church and Jews.

Back to the Fall Feasts. How can we know this idiom was what Jesus was getting at concerning His return?

Let's look at the holiday traditions and the ways God told the Children of Israel to celebrate these *moedim* back 1500 years before Yeshua came to fulfill the Spring Feasts.

YOM TERUAH
Remember the other names for this day? The Day of Shouting, the Day of Trumpets, *Yom Ha Din* (the Day of Judgment). It is the day the books are opened in heaven for judgment.

According to tradition, the last trumpet of *Teshuva* (40-day repentance period) is sounded on this day. If we pair that knowledge with this scripture, what do you see?

> **I Corinthians 15:51-52** Listen, I tell you a mystery: We will not all sleep, but we will all be changed—in a flash, in a twinkling of an eye, <u>at the last trumpet</u>. For the trumpet will sound, the <u>dead will be raised</u> imperishable, and we will all be changed.

This shouting and trumpets and rising from the dead is not some new concept that Paul was coming up with. Remember Paul's real name is Rabbi Sha'ul, and he is steeped in the knowledge of Judaism. He was teaching the Hebrew scriptures to the Corinthians here, from Isaiah and David

> **Isaiah 26:19** But your dead will live; their bodies will rise. You who dwell in the dust wake up and <u>shout for joy</u>. Your dew is like the dew of morning; the earth will give birth to her dead.

> **Psalm 81:3-4** Sound the ram's horn (shofar) at the New Moon, and when the moon is full, on the day of our festival; this is a decree for Israel, an ordinance of the God of Jacob.

Remember the three books that are opened in heaven on Yom Teruah? Some people are inscribed for righteousness, some for wickedness and the middle ground people are held in the balance from Yom Teruah until Yom Kippur, ten days later. If those in between are found worthy in that time frame, they are inscribed for life, if not, they are inscribed for destruction.

Daniel describes it this way:

Daniel 7:9-10 As I looked, thrones were set in place and the Ancient of Days took his seat. His clothing was white as snow...His throne was flaming with fire...Thousands upon thousands attended him...The court was seated, and the <u>books were opened</u>.

John describes it in Revelation like this:

Revelation 11:15-19 The seventh angel sounded his <u>trumpet</u>...Then God's temple in heaven was opened.

Jeremiah saw the same event and describes it like this:

Jeremiah 25:29-30 'I am calling down a sword on all who live on earth,' declares the Lord Almighty..."the Lord will <u>roar</u> from on high; he will <u>thunder</u> from his holy dwelling and <u>roar mightily</u> against his land. He will <u>shout</u> like those who tread the grapes, shout against all who live on the earth.

Here is another passage where Paul/Rabbi Shaul connects "the shout of Yom Teruah" with the resurrection and the rapture very clearly:

I Thessalonians 4:16-17 For the Lord himself shall descend from heaven with a <u>shout</u>, with the voice of the archangel, and with <u>trump</u> of God: and the dead in Christ shall rise first: Then we which are alive and remain shall be caught up together with them in the clouds, to meet the Lord in the air...

All these men's descriptions give context for Yeshua's words as recorded in Matthew:

Matthew 24:29-31 Immediately after the distress of those days...the peoples of the earth will mourn when they see the Son of God coming on the clouds of heaven with power and great glory. And he will send his angels with a loud <u>trumpet</u> call, and they will gather his elect from the four winds, from one end of the heavens to the other.

All this roaring and shouting and trumpets is Jesus coming back, as He promised! But not only that. Yom Teruah is also Rosh Hashanah, or head of the year. According to Jewish sages, the fundamental theme of Rosh Hashanah is God's coronation as King over us.

YOM TERUAH IS CORONATION DAY OF GOD AS KING! The Jewish sages teach that the world was created and then man was created on the date Tishrei 1. They believe that God is "sovereign over creation, *but His title of King was not appropriate until the creation of man because a King must have a people to govern.*"[1]

There is a story that describes Adam after he was made looking at all the beauty of the earth and the animals that had come to him to bow down to his authority, and Adam says, "Why are ye come to prostrate yourselves before me? Come, I and you, let us go and adorn in majesty and might, and acclaim as King over us the One who created us."[2] And so they did. Right then and there, they acclaimed their Creator as King over them. Then as in Psalm 93:1 they said, "The Lord reigns! He is appareled with majesty."

If you follow this rehearsal forward in time then, the first feast-related event in the last days timeline is that at the trumpet blast of Yom Teruah that year, Jesus will be crowned King of creation!

Daniel saw this event:

> **Daniel 7:13-14** "In my vision at night I looked, and there before me was one like a son of man, coming with the clouds of heaven. He approached the Ancient of Days and was led into his presence. [14] He was given authority, glory and sovereign power; all nations and peoples of every language worshiped him. His dominion is an everlasting dominion that will not pass away, and his kingdom is one that will never be destroyed.

151

John also records a vision what is going on in heaven simultaneously with the events on earth.

> **Revelation 11:15-17** The seventh angel sounded his trumpet, and there were loud voices in heaven, which said: "The kingdom of the world has become the kingdom of our Lord and of his Messiah, and he will reign for ever and ever." [16] And the twenty-four elders, who were seated on their thrones before God, fell on their faces and worshiped God, [17] saying: "We give thanks to you, Lord God Almighty, the One who is and who was, because you have taken your great power and have begun to reign."

Jesus will return to the earth with the blast of the trumpet and a shout, and He will be crowned King. But not by *all* people. This is the day the righteous are sealed for eternal life and the wicked are sealed for death.

WHO ARE THE RIGHTEOUS?[1] There are two groups, the "raptured" and the "resurrected." The first group is fairly self-explanatory. The raptured are those who are still alive at Yeshua's return on Yom Teruah and who have not taken the "mark of the beast" during the earth's tribulation.

> **I Thessalonians 4:15-17** According to the Lord's word, we tell you that we who are still alive, who are left until the coming of the Lord, will certainly not precede those who have fallen asleep. [16] For the Lord himself will come down from heaven, with a loud command, with the voice of the archangel and with the trumpet call of God, and the dead in Christ will rise first. [17] After that, we who are still alive and are left will be caught up together with them in the clouds to meet the Lord in the air. And so we will be with the Lord forever.

The resurrected people are the Believers in Jesus who have passed away in the last 2000+ years, including the martyrs who give up their lives at the end of the age, and Believers who had faith in God and in His Promised Messiah before Yeshua came.

> **Revelation 14:12-13** This calls for patient endurance on the part of the people of God who keep his commands and remain faithful to Jesus. [13] Then I heard a voice from heaven say, "Write this: Blessed are the dead who die in the Lord from now on." "Yes," says the Spirit, "they will rest from their labor, for their deeds will follow them."

WHO ARE THE WICKED?[1] The wicked who are marked for destruction are those who are still alive on Yom Teruah and align themselves and their actions with the anti-christ and his world order; those who took the "mark of the beast."

> **Revelation 14:9-10** A third angel followed them and said in a loud voice: "If anyone worships the beast and its image and receives its mark on their forehead or on their hand, [10] they, too, will drink the wine of God's fury, which has been poured full strength into the cup of his wrath. They will be tormented with burning sulfur in the presence of the holy angels and of the Lamb. [11] And the smoke of their torment will rise for ever and ever. There will be no rest day or night for those who worship the beast and its image, or for anyone who receives the mark of its name."

Included in the wicked group are those who already died not believing in the Promise of God's faithfulness (in the BC) of Yeshua and those who have already gone to their eternal deaths without declaring Jesus as Lord.

153

WHO'S LEFT? There is a third group of people who remain on earth on the Great Yom Teruah Day, the intermediates. People who don't believe in Jesus, but they also did not align with the anti-christ or take his mark. These folks are in for the ride of their lives. They obviously have some sense of right and wrong, enough to know not to climb aboard the anti-christ train. And they will have been living in opposition to anti-christ's new world-wide laws controlling everything from local travel and healthcare to the world food supply and energy for 3.5 years by the Great Yom Teruah.

These intermediates have ten days left to repent and get right with God. Those are the Ten Days of Awe between Yom Teruah and Yom Kippur, the Final Judgment Day. How do we know? Yom Kippur is the next Feast of the Lord coming and those ten days between feasts are pre-scribed introspection days, to be spent examining and repenting for sin in one's life.

DURING THE TEN DAYS OF AWE. These 10 days are described in Revelation. They are the most horrible in human history. During the 10 days the seven bowls of wrath are poured out on earth (Revelation 15 & 16).

From this we can see plainly that the events occur in this order. Revelation's books are opened in the temple in heaven and the angels come forth to pour out the wrath on the earth. The righteous, marked for eternal life, have already been taken into the clouds on Yom Teruah, however the wicked and the intermediates remain.

John's revelation was not the first telling of this devastating time. Isaiah writes five chapter's worth of description of the Last Days in Isaiah 24-29:8. Much of it describes the goodness of this time for the upright, but here are some important excerpts for the intermediates and wicked:

> **Isaiah 24:1, 3-6**: See, the LORD is going to lay waste the earth and devastate it; he will ruin its face and scatter its inhabitants...The earth will be completely laid waste and totally plundered. The LORD has spoken this word.
> [4] The earth dries up and withers, the world languishes and withers, the heavens languish with the earth. The earth is defiled by its people; they have disobeyed the laws, violated the statutes and broken the everlasting covenant. Therefore a curse consumes the earth; its people must bear their guilt. Therefore earth's inhabitants are burned up, and very few are left.

> **Isaiah 26:9-11**: When your judgments come upon the earth, the people of the world learn righteousness.[10] But when grace is shown to the wicked, they do not learn righteousness; even in a land of uprightness they go on doing evil and do not regard the majesty of the LORD. [11] LORD, your hand is lifted high, but they do not see it. Let them see your zeal for your people and be put to shame; let the fire reserved for your enemies consume them.

> **Isaiah 26:20-21** Go, <u>my people</u>, enter your rooms and shut the doors behind you; hide yourselves for a little while until his wrath has passed by. [21] See, the LORD is coming out of his dwelling to punish the people of the earth for their sins. The earth will disclose the blood shed on it; the earth will conceal its slain no longer.

Who is this "my people" referred to above? I believe they are the Jews who do not yet believe that Yeshua is Messiah. They are clinging to the old thoughts concerning a messiah and old rabbinical rulings that Jesus/Yeshua is not the Messiah. They will endure the devastation if they have not yet believed, however if they change their hearts during this horrific ten days, they can still live eternally with the God of Abraham, Isaac and Jacob and His Son, Yeshua.

Isaiah 26 answers some of the why questions of this devastation. The wicked have not learned uprightness through grace, but they have one last chance to learn through judgment. Their final decision is paramount!

A prototype of the bowls of wrath being poured out can be found in the story of the Exodus from Egypt. Though it will be much more devastating and worldwide than the 10 plagues poured out on Egypt.

YOM KIPPUR

As the final Day of Awe begins, so does the day of the final judgment. The holiest day. The Day of Atonement. It will fall, as always, on the 10th of Tishrei. Throughout history it has been celebrated and rehearsed as the day of Israel's national atonement. On this day, as the High Priests of old did, we will see Him face to face.

Zechariah makes a reference to seeing Jesus face to face using the "on that day" terminology and describing how the Nations have gathered against Jerusalem, firmly planting Zechariah's vision of future events in the final Last Days timeframe.

> **Zechariah 12:10** And I will pour out on the house of David and the inhabitants of Jerusalem a spirit of grace and supplication. They will look on me, the one they have pierced, and they will mourn for him as one mourns for an only child, and grieve bitterly for him as one grieves for a firstborn son.

Yom Kippur is the only day of the year when the High Priest enters the Most Holy place. It is the only day when the High Priest meets with God face to face. It fact, the people were not allowed to use the name of God because it was so holy. On Yom Kippur only, the High Priest alone could utter God's name before the people. The people would then fall prostrate before him in reverent fear. (They were worshipping the name of God not the High Priest!)

This picture of making Himself known to His people on Yom Kippur is the rehearsal of what is to come on Yom Kippur when Yeshua will make His identity known to Israel and all the earth!

WHITE GARMENTS. In the days of old, the Biblical command was for the priests to wear new white linen garments on this day.

> **Leviticus 16:2-4** Tell your brother Aaron that he is not to come whenever he chooses into the Most Holy Place behind the curtain in front of the atonement cover on the ark, or else he will die. For I will appear in the cloud over the atonement cover.
> [3] "This is how Aaron is to enter the Most Holy Place: He must first bring a young bull for a sin offering and a ram for a burnt offering. [4] He is to put on the sacred linen tunic, with linen undergarments next to his body; he is to tie the linen sash around him and put on the linen turban. These are sacred garments; so he must bathe himself with water before he puts them on.

One of the traditions that has sprung up is for the people of Israel to wear white clothing on Yom Kippur. Not a particular robe or anything, just a white dress or skirt and top or for the men white pants and a white dress shirt or even a white suit. One of the most beautiful sights in the world is to be outside the night of Yom Kippur in Jerusalem as all Israel is walking home from synagogue in the streets. (There is zero traffic as all commerce is halted for the day by national law.) Everyone is happy and chatting or singing; all dressed in white, they reflect the half moonlight. It is as if everyone is aglow!

This is a rehearsal of the day Yeshua returns and the armies of Heaven will be with him, dressed in white.

In John's Revelation he records seeing the Messiah and the armies of heaven (believers and angelic hosts) dressed in white on their way to the earth.

> **Revelation 19: 6-9; 11-14** Then I heard what sounded like a great multitude, like the roar of rushing waters and like loud peals of thunder, shouting: "Hallelujah! For our Lord God Almighty reigns. [7] Let us rejoice and be glad and give him glory! For the wedding of the Lamb has come, and his bride has made herself ready. [8] Fine linen, bright and clean, was given her to wear." (Fine linen stands for the righteous acts of God's holy people.)
> [9] Then the angel said to me, "Write this: Blessed are those who are invited to the wedding supper of the Lamb!" And he added, "These are the true words of God."
> [11] I saw heaven standing open and there before me was a white horse, whose rider is called Faithful and True. With justice he judges and wages war. [12] His eyes are like blazing fire, and on his head are many crowns. He has a name written on him that no one knows but he himself. [13] He is dressed in a robe dipped in blood, and his name is the Word of God. [14] The armies of heaven were following him, riding on white horses and dressed in fine linen, white and clean.

The people of Israel are rehearsing the wearing of white robes of righteousness every Yom Kippur Day until that Great Yom Kippur comes.

THE TWO GOATS. Remember the two goats that are chosen by lots? The Torah prescribes that one is "for the Lord" and becomes the sin-offering sacrifice for the priesthood, and the other goat is "for

Azazel" (alternate name for Satan) and receives the sin of Israel on its head, is led into the wilderness and pushed off a cliff into the abyss below.

Yeshua will fulfill this prescribed Yom Kippur rehearsal. John saw a vision of the fulfillment and recorded it.

> **Revelation. 20:1-3a** And I saw an angel coming down out of heaven, having the key to the Abyss and holding in his hand a great chain. [2] He seized the dragon, that ancient serpent, who is the devil, or Satan, and bound him for a thousand years. [3] He threw him into the Abyss, and locked and sealed it over him, to keep him from deceiving the nations anymore until the thousand years were ended.

The Jewish priesthood and people rehearsed this monumental event annually in the days of old. I don't think it has been reinstated since the re-gathering of the modern State of Israel.

THE JUDGMENT OR *NEILAH* (NOT THE GREAT WHITE THRONE JUDGMENT).
Traditionally, the final service on the last Day of Awe (Yom Kippur) is called *Neilah* meaning "locked." The title refers to the three books of Judgment (righteous, wicked or intermediate) which are closed and locked on this day as mankind, including Israel, remaining on earth is judged.

ISRAEL'S JUDGMENT is described:

> **Ezekiel 20:35-38** I will bring you into the wilderness of the nations and there, face to face, I will execute judgment upon you. [36] As I judged your ancestors in the wilderness of the land of Egypt, so I will judge you, declares the Sovereign LORD. [37] I will take note of you as you pass under my rod, and I will bring you into the bond of the covenant. [38] I will purge you of those who revolt and rebel against me. Although I will

159

bring them out of the land where they are living, yet they will not enter the land of Israel. Then you will know that I am the LORD.

Jeremiah 31:33-34 "This is the covenant I will make with the people of Israel after that time," declares the LORD. "I will put my law in their minds and write it on their hearts. I will be their God, and they will be my people. [34] No longer will they teach their neighbor, or say to one another, 'Know the LORD,' because they will all know me, from the least of them to the greatest," declares the LORD. "For I will forgive their wickedness and will remember their sins no more."

Romans 11:26-27 and in this way all Israel will be saved. As it is written: "The deliverer will come from Zion; he will turn godlessness away from Jacob. [27] And this is my covenant with them when I take away their sins."

When these prophecies are all read together with the teaching from Romans it is quite clear that Israel will realize that Yeshua is Messiah and all Israel will be saved!

THE INTERMEDIATES' JUDGMENT happens in silence. The nations and leaders of nations come before the Living God and are awe-struck.

Isaiah 52:14-15 Just as there were many who were appalled at him—his appearance was so disfigured beyond that of any human being and his form marred beyond human likeness—[15] so he will sprinkle many nations, and <u>kings will shut their mouths because of him</u>. For what they were not told, they will see, and what they have not heard, <u>they will understand</u>.

Yeshua's description of the separation of the sheep and the goats
(Matthew 25:31-46) is talking about the judgment on this Great Yom
Kippur Day.

> **Matthew 25: 31-32, 46** When the Son of Man comes
> in his glory, and all the angels with him, he will sit on
> his glorious throne. [32] All the nations will be gathered
> before him, and he will separate the people one from
> another as a shepherd separates the sheep from the
> goats. [33] He will put the sheep on his right and the
> goats on his left...[46] "Then they will go away to
> eternal punishment, but the righteous to eternal life."

It will be the hardest day on earth, both for those who are being
judged and Yeshua who is judging them.

> **John 3:16-17** For God so loved <u>the world</u> that he gave
> his one and only Son, that whoever believes in him
> shall not perish but have eternal life. [17] For God did
> not send his Son into the world to condemn the world,
> but to save the world through him.

God wants everyone! But even in the final hour, some will not choose
Him.

WHEN THE JUDGMENT TIME IS COMPLETE a worship service
like no other erupts! The One New Man has been created in fullness.
The new "Righteous Nation" consisting of literal Israel and Gentile
believers who came back with Jesus rejoice together.

Isaiah records it in prophecy:

> **Isaiah 26:1-2** In that day this song will be sung in the
> land of Judah: We have a strong city; God makes
> salvation its walls and ramparts. [2] Open the gates that
> the righteous nation may enter, the nation that keeps
> faith.

This worship service will conclude the Great Yom Kippur Day.
Psalm 47 will finally be fulfilled:

> Clap your hands, all you nations;
> shout to God with cries of joy.
> [2] For the LORD Most High is awesome,
> the great King over all the earth.
> [3] He subdued nations under us,
> peoples under our feet.
> [4] He chose our inheritance for us,
> the pride of Jacob, whom he loved.
> [5] God has ascended amid shouts of joy,
> the LORD amid the sounding of trumpets.
> [6] Sing praises to God, sing praises;
> sing praises to our King, sing praises.
> [7] For God is the King of all the earth;
> sing to him a psalm of praise.
> [8] God reigns over the nations;
> God is seated on his holy throne.
> [9] The nobles of the nations assemble
> as the people of the God of Abraham,
> for the kings of the earth belong to God;
> he is greatly exalted.

SUKKOT—THE FEAST OF TABERNACLES

Five days after Yom Kippur comes the final fall Feast of the Lord, Sukkot. It has been a rehearsal for the Wedding Feast of the Lamb! As far as I can tell, the Scriptures don't speak of what we should expect during the five days between Yom Kippur's judgment day and Sukkot's Wedding Feast. But the mood is drastically different. The Wedding Supper of the Lamb is the celebration to end all celebrations!

In rehearsal celebrations, Israel memorializes the time they spent in the wilderness, dependent solely on God, living in tents/booths/tabernacles. In Hebrew, the singular word for this tent is *sukkah*.

Sukkot is the plural form of that word. Sukkot also is the holiday which is a celebration of the final harvest of fruits and of the vine.

One of the ceremonies during Sukkot is the Drawing of Water. Each division of the priests had specific duties. 1. performed the sacrifices at the temple 2. went out into the Valley of Motzah to cut willow branches 3. Headed by the High Priest, drew water from the Pool of Siloam. These second and third delegations would "march back into the Temple simultaneously, one carrying willow branches as they swayed in the wind and the other carrying vases of water. A flutist called 'the pierced one' would lead the procession as the priests entered the Temple. These were symbolic of wind and water (Holy Spirit) coming to the Temple in the Messianic Age."[4]

The grand idea past, present, and future of Sukkot is that God will dwell with man! Because of this idea of "the dwelling of God with man" or "Immanuel," it is at this holy convocation of Sukkot, that many Biblical scholars place Yeshua's birth.

FUTURE SUKKOT CELEBRATIONS. The future of Sukkot or the Feast of Tabernacles as it is called in English, was prophesied in Zechariah as the time of year when all the nations of the world who had gathered against Israel would go up to Jerusalem to worship God together.

> **Zechariah 14:16-17** Then the survivors from all the nations that have attacked Jerusalem will go up year after year to worship the King, the LORD Almighty, and to celebrate the Festival of Tabernacles. [17] If any of the peoples of the earth do not go up to Jerusalem to worship the King, the LORD Almighty, they will have no rain.

This Feast of Tabernacles is the only Feast of the Lord specifically said to be celebrated during the Millennium Reign. In fact, did you

163

see that verse 17 above says that those nations not represented at the Feast of Sukkot in Jerusalem will suffer under the curse of a lack of rain. God takes this time very seriously!

CURRENT FEAST CELEBRATIONS. The Feast of Tabernacles has already been reinstated on a national level in Israel, though, unusually, not put on by the State of Israel. The International Christian Embassy Jerusalem (ICEJ) began hosting a celebration for Christians of the nations to come up to Jerusalem in 1980, and it has been going on year after year. "Up to 5,000 Christians from over 100 countries have come up to Jerusalem each year (regardless of the political climate in the Middle East) making the Feast of Tabernacles the largest and most popular annual Christian tourist event in Israel"[3] It is a week of spectacular worship, dynamic teaching, joyful playing and praying together, and bringing the financial resources of the world into Jerusalem.

THE EIGHTH DAY, THE LAST GREAT DAY. This holy day is an invitation by the Lord to an extra day of festivities because He is enjoying our company so much. Eight is the number of new beginnings, and it is right and good that the Millennial Reign be kicked off on the 8th Day. It is as if this new beginning of the new earth is picking up where the 7th day of God's Sabbath rest from creation left off so many millennia ago.

Oh, it's going to be great!

END NOTES

Major credit and kudos to Michael Cory for doing most of the primary research both in historical references and in the matching the scriptures to the stories for explanation and logically laying it out for this chapter over years of in-depth study. If you ever have the chance to catch one of his seminars in your area, GO! (or host one yourself!) www.voiceofjudah.com

1. Cory, Michael. 2012. Israel, the Church and the Kingdom. Voice of Judah International Ministries, Atlanta, GA. p.109

2. Hathi Trust Digital Library. "Pirke de Rabbi Eliezer" (the chapters of Rabbi Eliezer) Chapter XI, pp. 79-80. Retrieved June 28, 2013 from http://hdl.handle.net/2027/njp.32101062000755

3. ICEJ Feast of Tabernacles info can be found on their website. Quote retrieved July 2, 2013 from http://feast.icej.org/about

4. Cory, Michael. 2012. Israel, the Church and the Kingdom. Voice of Judah International Ministries, Atlanta, GA. p.120.

9

THE JEWISH SCHISM
AFTER YESHUA:
THE SPLIT BETWEEN MESSIANIC AND REGULAR JEWS
& THEN THE CHURCH AND MESSIANIC JEWS

After the Old Testament's record, there is a gap of 400 years of silence until Jesus showed up on the scene in quite a dramatic way for some Jews (angels singing and strange bright stars) and in a quiet way that was missed by most other Jews, even those who were watching for Him. Then the Bible records a flurry of stories and teachings by and about Jesus. Then it leaves us hanging, waiting for the end.

But the story of humanity doesn't stop and neither does the story of Jewish existence (both Jewish and Messianic in religion).

40-1000 AD
The Jews had scattered into the Roman Empire and had big communities all over. Some of these folks were still living outside the land of Israel from after the first Diaspora thanks to the Assyrian and Babylonian Empires. There were large concentrations of Jews residing in Rome and in Constantinople.

THE RISE OF CHRISTIANITY

In the beginning, all the followers of Jesus were Jewish. It was a Jewish sect called the *Netzarim*. But then it changed. What caused the split? It was gradual, no one woke up one morning and said, "Let's kick these pesky Jews out of their own religion, call ourselves Christians, and make it a Gentiles-only religion." However, we can look at the underlying issues that lead to the split between what we now refer to as Christianity and Judaism. This split is also related to the split between "still-waiting-for-Messiah" Jews and Messianic Jews (Netzarim).

If we assume the resurrection occurred around the year 30 AD, for the first seven years the Gospel had been limited to the Jewish people, until the God-fearing Roman Gentile Cornelius from Caesarea got hold of the message via Shimon (Simon in English, but you probably know him as Peter).[1]

Acts 10 tells the whole story, but here is the best part for Gentiles:

> **Acts 10:34-36** Then Peter opened *his* mouth and said: "In truth I perceive that God shows no partiality. [35] But every nation whoever fears Him and works righteousness is accepted by Him. [36] The word which *God* sent to the children of Israel, preaching peace through Jesus Christ—He is Lord of all.

Life in Israel continued on after Cornelius and his whole household were baptized in water and spoke in tongues (Acts 10:46), but the Gospel was still only being preached to the Jews, according to Acts 11:19b, which says, "…preaching the word to no one but the Jews only." But then word started getting out, beginning with some Jews from Cyprus and Cyrene who preached to some Hellenists in Antioch (Acts 11:20-21). There were influential, prophetic Jews who also began preaching in Antioch. These included Barnabas, Simeon,

Manaen and Sha'ul. By the time the events of Acts 13 roll around, Sha'ul and Barnabas were set apart for a specific work for the Lord, and they were anointed by the believers there and begin teaching all over about Yeshua the Jewish Messiah (Acts 13:1-4).

More and more Gentiles came to believe in Yeshua, and Rabbi Sha'ul and Barnabas continued from town to town probably following a similar pattern as is described below:

> **Acts 13:14-16** NKJV But when they (Paul & his party) departed from Perga, they came to Antioch in Pisidia, and went into the synagogue on the Sabbath day and sat down. [15] And after the reading of the Law and the Prophets, the rulers of the synagogue sent to them, saying, "Men *and* brethren, if you have any word of exhortation for the people, say on."
> [16] Then Paul stood up, and motioning with *his* hand said, "Men of Israel, and you who fear God, listen:

This event probably occurred early in the 40's AD. Antioch in Pisidia is present-day south-central Turkey. Paul is referring to a Jewish synagogue there. There was a mixture of people who met together in the synagogues outside Israel. Paul was speaking to three distinct groups of people: Jews, Gentile God-fearers (like Cornelius), and Gentile Proselytes (converts to Judaism).

WHO WERE THESE PEOPLE WORSHIPPING GOD TOGETHER IN THE SYNAGOGUE?

During that time and from even earlier in the second century BC under the Macabee's rule, the Jewish religion was very evangelistic in its outlook. The God-fearers were allowed to hang out with the Jews, even though they had not converted, as long as they repudiated idolatry.[1] But the goal of the Jewish leaders was to see them become Jewish. The Jews even did some forcible conversions to Judaism (something they are a bit ashamed of and don't talk about).[3] Once the Gentile God-fearers converted they were called Proselytes.

This is not unlike the way our churches function today: non-Christians are welcome to come and worship with us; they can check out this "Christian thing," all with *our* underlying goal or hope of seeing them added to the Kingdom of God.

So the synagogues abroad were made up of three types of people: Jews, Proselytes, and Gentile God-fearers. The God-fearers were treated as a lower class of people and were not allowed to participate in certain practices because they had not (yet) converted to Judaism. Even after they converted there were some practices that were held for Jews by birth alone, such as serving in the priesthood (the Cohenim). However, converts were allowed to serve as rabbis. But there were restrictions on who could be married to whom and how the sons of those marriages could serve.[2]

Those restrictions were not done to be mean or discriminatory against intermarriage, but to try to maintain in the priesthood a purity and holiness (set apart for a specific purpose) dictated by the Torah in:

> **Deuteronomy 7:3-4, 6** Nor shall you make marriages with them. You shall not give your daughter to their son, nor take their daughter for your son. [4] For they will turn your sons away from following Me, to serve other gods; so the anger of the LORD will be aroused against you and destroy you suddenly… [6]"For you *are* a holy people to the LORD your God; the LORD your God has chosen you to be a people for Himself, a special treasure above all the peoples on the face of the earth.

SOME HEBREW LANGUAGE BACKGROUND

The word *proselyte* as used in the scripture referred to a male convert to Judaism. Proselyte is translated from the Hebrew word *"ger"* (pronounced like Gary, not Jerry, because there is no J sound in Hebrew). *Ger* (*Gerim* is the plural) is derived from the Hebrew word *L'gar* (spelled: lamed, gimmel, resh) which means "to sojourn (with)" or "to reside." It was during the 200's-800's AD that the word came to be understood more as a convert to Judaism than a sojourner.[3] According to Rabbi Marc Angel, "When the Torah commands compassion and equal justice for the *ger*, it is referring to these 'residents.'"[4]

BACK TO RABBI SHA'UL/PAUL'S STORY. So when Paul was asked to speak in the synagogue, the three types of people there had no idea what they were asking for! Over the next few minutes, Paul taught them all from the Torah, describing the Messiah and then testified that the long-awaited Messiah had come in the person of Yeshua!

Acts 13:42-48 tells what happened after that.

> [42] So when the Jews went out of the synagogue, the Gentiles begged that these words might be preached to them the next Sabbath. [43] Now when the congregation had broken up, <u>many of the Jews and devout proselytes followed Paul and Barnabas, who, speaking to them, persuaded them to continue in the grace of God.</u>
> [44] On the next Sabbath almost the whole city came together to hear the word of God. [45] But <u>when the Jews saw the multitudes, they were filled with envy;</u> and contradicting and blaspheming, they opposed the things spoken by Paul. [46] Then Paul and Barnabas grew bold and said, "It was necessary that the word of God should be spoken to you first; but since you reject it, and judge yourselves unworthy of everlasting life, behold, we turn to the Gentiles. [47] For so the Lord has commanded us:

> I have set you as a light to the Gentiles,
> That you should be for salvation to the ends of the
> earth.'" (referring to Isaiah 46:9)
> [48] Now <u>when the Gentiles heard this, they were glad</u>
> and glorified the word of the Lord. And as many as
> had been appointed to eternal life believed.

So it is very plain that Jews and others were interested in what Paul had to say—whether or not they believed in Yeshua at this point is not stated—but they were interested! This leaves at least two questions: Why were the Jews envious and opposed to Paul's speech? Why were the Gentiles glad?

The Two Questions

Then the Jewish leaders began to run into a problem. Second class treatment aside, these Jews were upset because Paul's teaching was undermining the Jewish community they were building. The community of Jews, in order to be successful among the nations especially in the Roman Empire, needed numbers. To get numbers, they needed converts. The Jews made up 10% of the Roman Empire.[1] Their numbers were growing because of converts to Judaism. The more people who were part of Judaism, the more influence they would have with Roman government.[1] For the Jews who were living outside Israel, conversion was not just theological, it was political. As usual, when mixing religion and politics a royal mess developed.

Then Paul came along and said people don't have to be Jewish to be accepted in the Kingdom of God. Unfortunately for the Jews, being part of the Kingdom of God, and being accepted by the God of Israel had been the bait they were using to reel the Gentiles into Judaism! Now the Jews were envious of Paul and his teachings because they were losing the ability to bring more Gentiles into their Jewish community! Obviously not every Jew was having a hard time with this teaching, but these Jews we are talking about could have been either Messianic or regular in their beliefs, there is no specification in scripture.

Why were the Gentiles happy? That's pretty simple now: They got to be accepted into the Kingdom of God, and received equality with the Jews in standing before God, without having to follow all the Jewish rules. They were elevated to "first class status" in their congregations without converting to Judaism. The Gentiles then became a wedge issue between the Jewish community and the Messianic community. It may surprise you, but the major wedge between these two Jewish groups was *not* Yeshua, it was these Gentile converts that were not added to Judaism, but got to be in on God's promises and His Kingdom!

There were all kinds of factions of Jewish groups teaching all sorts of things within the body of Judaism at that time: Pharisees, Sadducees, Essenes, Zealots, Scarii, Netzarim (or Nazarenes). The Netzarim (Messianic Jews) were accepted as just another sect of Judaism.[7] No problem. All the groups were wrestling to become the leaders and most widely accepted among worldwide Jewry. But with Sha'ul's teaching, the Nazarenes were seen in Jewish eyes as trying to lure away the Gentiles with fewer restrictions to follow than Judaism and still be accepted by the God of Israel. This became the beginning of the problems.

STRUCTURE OF THE EARLY MESSIANIC COMMUNITY

The Sanhedrin (meaning "the 70") was the ruling body of Jews; they were not Messianic, unless there were a secret few Netzarim among them. The Sanhedrin had a ruler called the *Naci* whose lineage must be of the line of David. I presume that is because of the ruling nature of this position, especially in light of there being no Jewish king in Israel.

The Messianic community was ruled by the Jerusalem Council. The head of the Jerusalem Council was also a *Naci,* and James was the first one, and he functioned in this position during the following debate. (Later this position became referred to as the Bishop of Jerusalem). James was Yeshua's brother, therefore also in the line of David. The Messianic community of believers was formatted just like the regular Jewish ruling body or government. The Jerusalem Council continued to be the governing body of Believers even into the early church years. It was headed by a Jewish man, in the line of David, until the Bar Kochba Rebellion in 135 AD.[1]

THE SPLIT

The split between Jews and Messianic Jews began in the year 50 AD with that major debate that arose in this Messianic community. They wanted to know, "What do we do with all these Gentiles that have become followers of Messiah Yeshua?" "Should they convert to Judaism or not?" And the Jewish Believers in Yeshua were split in their opinion.

Acts 15 tells the story and the resolution that was brought about at the Council of Jerusalem between the apostles and elders and Paul and Barnabas.

> **Acts 15:1-2, 4-5, 7-11, 18-20, 27-29** And certain *men* came down from Judea and taught the brethren, "Unless you are circumcised according to the custom of Moses, you cannot be saved." [2] Therefore, when Paul and Barnabas had no small dissension and dispute with them, they determined that Paul and Barnabas and certain others of them should go up to Jerusalem, to the apostles and elders, about this question. [4] And when they had come to Jerusalem, they were received by the church and the apostles and the elders; and they reported all things that God had done with them. [5] But some of the sect of the Pharisees who believed rose up, saying, "It

is necessary to circumcise them, and to command *them* to keep the law of Moses."

[7] And when there had been much dispute, Peter rose up *and* said to them: "Men *and* brethren, you know that a good while ago God chose among us, that by my mouth the Gentiles should hear the word of the gospel and believe. [8] So God, who knows the heart, acknowledged them by giving them the Holy Spirit, just as *He did* to us, [9] and made no distinction between us and them, purifying their hearts by faith. [10] Now therefore, why do you test God by putting a yoke on the neck of the disciples which neither our fathers nor we were able to bear? [11] But we believe that through the grace of the Lord Jesus Christ we shall be saved in the same manner as they."

(James says) "Known to God from eternity are all His works. [19] Therefore I judge that we should not trouble those from among the Gentiles who are turning to God, [20] but that we write to them to abstain from things polluted by idols, *from* sexual immorality, *from* things strangled, and *from* blood.

[27] We have therefore sent Judas and Silas, who will also report the same things by word of mouth. [28] For it seemed good to the Holy Spirit, and to us, to lay upon you no greater burden than these necessary things: [29] that you abstain from things offered to idols, from blood, from things strangled, and from sexual immorality. If you keep yourselves from these, you will do well."

So the Naci of the Messianic Jewish community, James, was the one who made the ruling on the question of the Gentiles. The Gentile will only be required to keep four laws pertaining to Judaism:
1. abstain from things offered to idols
2. no sexual immorality
3. no strangled things
4. no blood

What is interesting though is that all four of these laws are actually referring to one thing. Gentiles were to worship only one God. By following those four laws the Jews could see that they were not worshiping idols, because those four things were all related to the idol worship in pagan temples practiced at that time. Pagan worship involved strangling animal sacrifices, drinking blood of both humans and animals, and having sex with temple prostitutes and others. The main concern of the Messianic Believers was making sure that the Gentiles were proving that they only worshipped one God and the one God they worshipped was the God of Israel.[1]

THE SPLIT WIDENS

It was very attractive to be a Jew in the Roman Empire. They received a special status and special schools, a special kind of government, special community, even a special commercial status throughout the entire Roman Empire. There was definite economic benefit to being a Jew, but things changed with the 135 AD Bar Kochba Rebellion. After that Jewish revolt, persecutions started against the Jews in the Roman Empire.

So the gap that began with the differing answers to the question of what to do with the Gentiles, widened the split that was occurring between the Jews and Messianic Jews during the Bar Kochba Rebellion. Until then Messianic Believers had been considered part of the Jewish world, including those who were Gentile Believers, even by the Romans.

There were still Gentiles coming into the Messianic community, but then it was not so attractive be associated with the Jews...they were getting persecuted! Being Jewish becomes negative, almost overnight.

Another factor soon increased this ever widening gap between Jews and Messianic Jews: A new prayer was added to the Jewish life, to be spoken three times daily. There were 18 benedictions in the Jewish world, which are still used today. They are blessings of the Lord, and then appeals to Him. At *Yavneh*, the Jewish leaders added this new benediction to the prayer called the *Berkat HaMinim* (which means "curse against the heretics"). This was done by the rabbis and Pharisees who were trying to form a new Judaism that was more in their stream of thinking. Remember all the Jewish groups earlier that were fighting for pre-eminence among themselves? This was still the same issue. It was likely that the target of this new benediction was the Sadducees, with a goal of removing them from the Jewish Community.[1]

> The Birkat haMinim as it appears today reads: And for slanderers let there be no hope, and let all wickedness perish as in a moment; let all thine enemies be speedily cut off, and the dominion of arrogance do you uproot and crush, cast down and humble speedily in our days. Blessed are you, YHVH, who breakest the enemies and humbles the arrogant.[7]

An old copy of the *Birkat haMinim* found at the Cairo Genizah reads:[7]

> For the renegades let there be no hope, and may the arrogant kingdom soon be rooted out in our days, and the Netzarim and the Minim perish as in a moment and be blotted out from the book of life and with the righteous may they not be inscribed. Blessed are you, YHVH, who humbles the arrogant.

That is some very strong language! Unfortunately, because this new benediction was said three times daily, it was definitely applied in practice to the Nazarene Community. They could not curse themselves three times daily, so the Nazarenes were being removed from the Jewish community at the same time as the Sadducees.

This rejection was not just a social problem for the Netzarim, but a huge economic problem, because if this group was no longer "allowed to be Jewish," they couldn't receive the special benefits and protection offered to the Jewish people by the Roman Empire. It also became a huge theological problem years down the road, even to today. The Netzarim, the ones doing right, *receiving* the light of Yeshua to *be* the light of Yeshua to the world, were now rejected by their blood brothers, the Jews, and isolated by their spiritual brothers, who changed their name to Christians instead of Nazarenes.

Many Nazarenes, Messianic Believers, chose to go back to their old faith because they had suddenly been cast into poverty with this rejection. They had a dilemma of food or Yeshua, and they went with food. This decision was likely what the book of Hebrews is about, encouraging Messianic Believers to keep the faith. "You are suffering, but so did your forefathers the prophets, hang in there!" This Messianic community was being isolated and targeted by the growing Pharisee Community, ever widening the gap between the two.[1]

ANOTHER UPRISING IN ISRAEL, 67-70 AD

Another Jewish revolt began in 67 AD, and the Jews actually won against Rome's Gallus and the "floundering XII (regiment) was forced to retreat from Jerusalem. The initial triumph over the Romans encouraged Jewish masses, many of which construed the turn of events in their favor as a signal that Providence was shining upon them and giving them miraculous favor—finally."[8] The Messianics saw this win as the beginning of the end and were sure that the Second Coming was on its way. The Jews saw it much the same, except they were just looking for the first coming of the Messiah. Eschatology was the watch-word of the day!

However, Rome couldn't let the black mark of an uprising against the mighty Roman Empire rest, so they sent Vespasian to mop up the mess.

Yeshua had ascended about 40 years earlier when the might of Rome swept down from the north, through the Galilee region and on toward

Jerusalem. The remaining disciples must have recalled a day sitting on a hillside overlooking Jerusalem talking with Yeshua the Good Shepherd when He said,

> **Luke 21:20-22** "But when you see Jerusalem surrounded by armies, then know that its desolation is near. [21] Then let those who are in Judea flee to the mountains, let those who are in the midst of her depart, and let not those who are in the country enter her. [22] For these are the days of vengeance, that all things which are written may be fulfilled."

So when the Messianics heard from escaping Galilean refugees that the Roman Army was coming to surround Jerusalem, some left for the mountains of Jordan. According to Michael Lederer, "Vibrations from the Roman armies' approaching drum beats created no little stir amongst the Jewish people—*prompting mass evacuations,* even before the great eschatological war was officially contested and decided in Jerusalem."[8]

Some of those folks who headed out were part of the Messianic community who were heeding Yeshua's warning, "get out while the gettin's good" (paraphrase, obviously). Whether the majority of the Messianic Believers, including The Council of Jerusalem left before Rome arrived or surrendered to the Roman soldiers and were relocated is of some dispute.[8] However, where they ended up is not: It was the mountains of Pella, Jordan, where many lived in caves. Simon, a cousin of Yeshua, became the new Naci of the Council of Jerusalem (after James was martyred), and he was the one leading the people to Pella. Things were not going well in Jerusalem. The Zealots from the north were the main escapees, and when they came into Jerusalem they were not at all pleased with the way the Sanhedrin was running things. The Zealots felt Jerusalem's Pharisaic leaders were too moderate, and so they began killing anyone less fanatical than

179

themselves. They even burned a food stockpile that could have kept Jerusalem going for many years' worth of Roman siege.

Lederer struggled with the question of whether the Messianic community leaving Jerusalem was a betrayal to their brothers, and decided, "Definitely not! 'Internal upheavals lead to the departure of many disconcerted Jews, as frenzied and murderous Zealots usurped power in Jerusalem and took control of the struggle (*Wars*, 4.377). They would have particularly threatened Jewish believers in Yeshua/Jesus, when those 'assassins' took over the city...'' [8]

While the Messianics were not accused of betraying their Jewish brothers by leaving Jerusalem (How many were left after the Zealots and Romans were finished anyway?), it certainly did not go a long way toward bettering already broken relations between the groups. Those who went to Pella returned and were a presence around Jerusalem until at minimum the second century.[8]

את

POLARIZING WRITINGS

Another blow to knock the Jews and Messianic Jews further apart came in the form of some writings from the Gentile believers. The first truly anti-Semitic writing that appeared was called *The Epistle of Barnabas*. It was written around 96-98 AD.[5] There was a lot of writing actually going on at this time in history, and some of it is pseudepigraphal, or "false writings." Writing that is attributed to someone (usually with credentials or first-hand knowledge of the subject) who didn't write it, but whose name lends credibility to it. *The Epistle of Barnabas* is one of those. It is claimed that Barnabas wrote it, but he did not. It was influential in the newly forming

Church (Gentile believers who were rejecting the Jewishness of the Netzarim), however it was never considered official church doctrine.

The Epistle of Barnabas says that the Jews lost their Covenant forever when Moses destroyed the tablets on Mount Sinai.[6] It claims that Jesus is for the Gentiles who are the true recipients of God's Covenant, not the Jews. In the very first chapter the keeping of the new moon festivals and the Sabbaths are abolished as well as other Jewish laws for Christians.[6] And by chapter five, there is only one law, the "Law of Jesus Christ."

IGNATIUS

The divisive wedges were ever widening between the Jews and Messianic Jews, and the next blow drove further separation between Messianic Jews and Gentile Believers: the Bishop Ignatius of Antioch who lived at the same time as Polycarp, a disciple of John. Ignatius was the first major church writer to write something against the Jews. Ignatius said, "If we conform to Judaism then we have not received grace." He encouraged his followers not to observe the Sabbath, but to worship on "the Lord's day" the day of the resurrection. He said, "It is absurd to have Jesus Christ on the lips and at the same time live like a Jew." This was around 105 AD, and the complete severance between Judaism and Christianity was well on its way.[1]

This divide became an identity crisis like no other, because the Gentile believers started trying to find their identity apart from the Jewish people, which God never intended to happen! It was the lack of true identity that lead to some horrible decisions in the 2nd and 3rd centuries for the early Church. Since those decisions were foundational to the Church, they got carried in our DNA as a body of believers. Most of these decisions were wildly anti-Semitic which was (and is) a huge problem—both for the Jews and for the Christians.

181

100-200 AD

There were still Jews throughout the Roman Empire and the rest of the known world, and they were still discovering Yeshua as their Messiah, just not in numbers as great as they had been in the previous century. The major Jewish communities were located in Alexandria in northern Africa, southern Greece, western and central-southern Turkey, Syria, Judea, Babylon, Cyprus, and Rome.[1] The early Christian growth was located in the same places, both Jews coming to Yeshua and Gentile God-fearers latching onto the hope of Yeshua. The hearts of the Gentile God-fearers were already prepared by the Torah teachings in the synagogues where they attended Shabbat services and prayer.

As time went by, the Jews began treating the Gentile believers in Yeshua as second class citizens. So where it had been an attraction for Gentile believers to meet with the Jews, it became a negative factor to be part of the Jewish community. So the Gentile believers began forming their own meeting houses. So, when the Gentiles came to faith and then had an identity crisis and turned away from their Jewish brothers, the Christianity that formed became an increasingly anti-Semitic faith.

BAR KOCHBA REVOLT OF 137 AD, BACK IN ISRAEL

Around 118 AD Hadrian became the Emperor of Rome, and he was sympathetic to the Jews. He allowed them back into Jerusalem and promised them they could rebuild the temple. The Jews got very excited at this prospect and began making plans and saving money. Then Hadrian changed his mind and told the Jews to find another site for their temple and began deporting some of them to North Africa.

This did not go over so well with the Jews and secretly, they began preparing for a revolt. By 123 AD, they were making surprise guerrilla attacks on the Roman Army, and having a bit of success, but then Hadrian sent another legion into Judea to "deal with the terrorism."

About this time a man named Simon Bar Kochba arose among the Jewish people. His leadership brought the people together in a new revolt against Rome where they captured 50 strongholds and 985 unsecured towns in Judea.[10] He happened to be from the line of David and he was functioning like the "conquering king" that the Jews were looking for in a messiah. Many Jews were calling him a messiah too.

Hadrian was fed up with the rebellious behavior of the Jews and was "compelled to summon the greatest general of his time, Julius Severus, from Britain, to conduct the campaign against the Jews"[11] and put a stop to the revolt. The Jews fled to Bethar, Bar Kochba's headquarters. Militarily, Bethar was perfectly positioned as a stronghold from which to launch attacks, but in 135 AD, on the 9th of Av, Bethar was swept up by Hadrian's forces. Every Jew in Bethar was killed; sources say over half a million Jews died in this battle at Bethar.[11] Hadrian then sold into slavery other Jews he rounded up who had not participated in Bar Kochba's Revolt. Hadrian renamed the country from Judea to Syria Palestina and began to build a new city over the top of the old plowed Jerusalem. He named the new city after himself *Aelia Capitolina*. On the temple mount, Hadrian build a new temple to Jupiter, and the Jews were forbidden to enter Jerusalem except on one day per year to mourn the loss of their temple, the 9th of Av.

The Bar Kochba Revolt officially separated the Messianic community from the regular Jews because they claimed Bar Kochba was the messiah, and the Messianic Jews said, "No, he is not," and then they did not come to fight along side the regular Jews. This lack of support seems to have been the last straw for the regular Jews, and they no longer accepted the Natzarim as a sect of Judaism.

This Jewish Bar Kochba Revolt against the Romans became the end of the Council of Jerusalem too.[1]

The split was complete. The Jews who believed Yeshua was the Messiah were considered heretics among the Jews, and James' ruling that the Gentile believers should only have to follow the Jewish no-idolatry laws lead to the Christians rejecting the Jews—who brought them the Gospel—from amongst them *because* the Jews followed the Torah (as commanded by the God they both worshiped!) It makes NO SENSE!

From my 20/20 perspective, pride on both sides seems to be the underlying root in this split. The Messianic Jews were proud to be Jews and follow the Torah, and treated Gentile Christians with a second-class status, if not distain. The Gentiles were proud because they were "free from the Law of Torah" and living with a "higher revelation." They treated the Jews who did follow the Law as if they were bound in sin.

And it only got worse from there.

THEOLOGICAL FATHERS BEGAN TO WRITE IN THE 130'S[1]

Justin Martyr was first. He is considered the father of Christian Theology and all churches believed/accepted what Martyr wrote: *I and II Apologies*. The two main competitions for Christianity at this time were Judaism and the Roman and Greek gods. Martyr argued for the distinction among the two groups, and he discussed a series of issues.

Martyr looked at the Hebrew scriptures (the New Testament had not been gathered or canonized yet) and decided there were four important episodes in Biblical history that define what Christians believed:

A. Creation: Everything was created in God's order. Perfection! (Genesis 1-2)

B. The Fall: Adam and Eve took the fruit against God's instruction and sin corrupted the world. (Genesis 3)

C. The Redemption in Christ: The most important event ever.

D. Return of Christ: The Grande Finale when God will rule over all things.

All Christian churches believed these things; they were all taken from the Hebrew scriptures. But Martyr jumped from the beginning of Genesis in A and B to the New Testament in C. So what about the WHOLE rest of the Bible? Martyr tried to explain it by saying that there was value in the rest of the Hebrew scriptures only in that they pointed to Christ's coming or they pointed to the hardness of Jewish hearts, and there was some Hebrew scripture, like the moral code that was good and binding for all men. The rest was worthless.

What happens when we compare Justin Martyr's teachings above to what Yeshua said about the Hebrew scriptures? There is no agreement whatsoever! Basically Martyr removed the Jews from importance in the scripture. There is no Exodus, no Mount Sinai, no prophets, no Torah. Yeshua on the other hand, quoted the Hebrew scriptures and basically said, "You remember that you're not supposed sin by doing this or that, well, I will take it a step further: don't even allow your heart to consider sinning."

> **Luke 6:27-31** "But I say to you who hear: Love your enemies, do good to those who hate you, [28] bless those who curse you, and pray for those who spitefully use you. [29] To him who strikes you on the *one* cheek, offer the other also. And from him who takes away your cloak, do not withhold *your* tunic either. [30] Give to everyone who asks of you. And from him who takes away your goods do not ask *them* back. [31] And just as

185

you want men to do to you, you also do to them likewise.

Matthew 5:17-21 "Do not think that I came to destroy the Law or the Prophets. I did not come to destroy but to fulfill. [18] For assuredly, I say to you, till heaven and earth pass away, one jot or one tittle will by no means pass from the law till all is fulfilled. [19] Whoever therefore breaks one of the least of these commandments, and teaches men so, shall be called least in the kingdom of heaven; but whoever does and teaches *them,* he shall be called great in the kingdom of heaven. [20] For I say to you, that unless your righteousness exceeds *the righteousness* of the scribes and Pharisees, you will by no means enter the kingdom of heaven.
[21] "You have heard that it was said to those of old, 'You shall not murder, and whoever murders will be in danger of the judgment.' [22] But I say to you that whoever is angry with his brother without a cause shall be in danger of the judgment. And whoever says to his brother, 'Raca!' shall be in danger of the council. But whoever says, 'You fool!' shall be in danger of hell fire.

There is nothing similar between what Martyr pushes forward as foundational Church ideas and what Jesus taught! Yikes!

Justine Martyr also wrote a letter while in Ephesus to Trypho the Jew (who was escaping the Bar Kochba Rebellion in the late 130's) and in the letter Martyr tried to explain that Jesus was the Jewish Messiah to this Jewish man using the prophets and Hebrew scriptures.[15] Trypho said only a moron would believe such a thing.[1] They debated back and forth some and then Justin Martyr called the Gentile Church the "true spiritual Israel."[15] And this became a very significant statement of untruth!

REPLACEMENT THEOLOGY WAS BORN

It was in this statement of Martyr's debate that Replacement Theology was birthed. And boy was it a nasty seed for Jews and Christians since it has grown to its full poison fruit!

The thought process that follows this statement that the Church is the true spiritual Israel is that everything that God promised to the Jewish people and to Israel really belongs to the Church. Replacement Theology says that the Church has replaced Israel in God's mission and plan and promises. Martyr said that "Christianity has God's climaxes for all of creation"[1] and "God's relationships with the physical descendants of the Jews ends, and now begins with the spiritual descendants, the Church."[1] In reference to the Bar Kochba Rebellion, Martyr shockingly said about circumcision (Remember, it is *God's* appointed sign of His Covenant):

> The purpose of this (circumcision) was that you and only you might suffer the afflictions that are now justly yours; that only your land be desolated, and you(r) cities ruined by fire, that the fruits of you(r) land be eaten by strangers before your very eyes; that not one of you be permitted to enter your city of Jerusalem. Your circumcision of the flesh is the only mark by which you can certainly be distinguished from other men...as I stated before it was by reason of your sins and the sins of your fathers that, among other precepts, God imposed upon you the observance of the sabbath as a mark.[13]

Where circumcision was meant by God to be a sign of His favor over a people, Martyr called it the sign of God's rejection! That is a really twisted lie of the enemy there, and it was sown into the foundation of the Church's accepted doctrine!

The Church then constructed from Martyr's writings a theology where the Jews were essentially absent...and ultimately became the enemies.[1]

MARCION AND GNOSTICISM BLEED INTO CHURCH FOUNDATIONS

Then, there was a major philosophy prevalent in the world, Gnosticism. Even Rabbi Sha'ul refers to it in his writing. Gnosticism is the separation of spiritual and material worlds. It claims that the material world is a reflection of the spiritual world. It began to influence the early church, lead by Marcion, (pronounced MAR-ze-in) around the year 200. He argued that there are actually two Gods: a God of the Old Testament and a God of the New Testament. And the God of the New Testament was greater. The old God pertained exclusively to the material realm and new God to the spiritual realm. Marcion's take on Christianity is that Jesus rescued us from the material world...and from the Jews.

TERTULLIAN

Two major Church theologians responded and ultimately defeated Marcion. First was Tertullian. He argued for the unity of God. The God of Jesus Christ was the God of Abraham, Isaac and Jacob. No other God! But then Tertullian had to explain the unity of the Scripture. How do you go from the Old to the New, because there seems to be a huge difference in the way God is portrayed? Tertullian said, "The commandments of the Torah are degrading and unworthy of an enlightened people. They were given to Jews to curb idolatry and greed, which is unique to them and it's not shared by the rest of the human race"[1] (yeah, right!) "Their trail of crimes culminated in the killing of Christ. Jews were always unworthy of election and now they've lost it. God's choice is now transferred to the Gentiles who are capable of living at a higher level than the Jews."[9] These are just sick thoughts, and they were being accepted by the early Church.

Here are some direct quotes from Tertullian's writings:

> "(W)e neither accord with the Jews in their peculiarities in regard to food, nor in their sacred days, nor even in their well-known bodily sign, nor in the possession of a common name, which surely behoved to be the case if we did homage to the same God as they."

> "The sacred writers withal, in giving previous warning of these things, all with equal clearness ever declared that, in the last days of the world, God would, out of every nation, and people, and country, choose for Himself more faithful worshippers, upon whom He would bestow His grace, and that indeed in ampler measure, in keeping with the enlarged capacities of a nobler dispensation."

> "It was the merited punishment of their sin not to understand the Lord's first advent: for if they had, they would have believed; and if they had believed, they would have obtained salvation."[9]

Tertullian's pride-filled ideas about the Jews were embedded into foundational Church doctrine. He wasn't trying to attack the Jews; he was just responding to Marcion's idea that there were two Gods.

IRENAEUS

The other responder to Marcion was Irenaeus. He said there was "a singular theme beginning with creation and (running) all the way to the consummation that God works from beginning to end through redemption."[1] But he still had to explain the Jews to the Gentile Church, so he said, "God chose the Jews in order to prepare them for Christ. But they rejected and murdered Him. Because the Jews rejected Him, God granted their inheritance to Gentiles alone. Jews who boast of being Israel are being disinherited from the grace of God. They are no longer useful."[1]

With their acceptance of Irenaeus' statement "Jews are no longer useful" the early Church leaders set into motion all the diabolical things that have happened to the Jews over the 2000 years since Yeshua! Ugh!

ESUEBIUS, CHURCH HISTORIAN IN 300 AD

Things went from bad to worse. The young Church was on the wrong trajectory! Esuebius was a church historian from around 300 AD, and his account of history, *The Ecclesiastical History*, is still used in seminaries today. He actually talked about the Netzarim, the Messianic Jewish community, as large Jewish keeping-the-Torah-and-believing-in-Jesus groups that were still holding together in Palestine, Cyprus, Mesopotamia and Syria.

Esuebius said, "Judaism has no merit and is a threat to the church."[1] He accused the Jews of crucifying Christians at Purim (Esther's holiday) to show their rejection of Jesus. This accusation became embedded into his historical account, and in a thousand years became a basis for the "ritual murder charges" and "blood libel charges" that swept Europe, stirring up major anti-Semitism and leading to the killings of thousands and thousands of Jews anywhere these accusations were laid.

CLEMENTINE RECOGNITIONS

About this time the Clementine Recognitions came into play. In order to become a Christian, a person had to make a number of renouncements, called the Clementine Recognitions. "I renounce the whole worship of the Hebrews, circumcision, all its legalisms, unleavened bread, Passover, the sacrificing of lambs, the Feast of Weeks, Jubilees, the Trumpets, Atonement, Tabernacles and all the other Hebrew feasts, sacrifices, prayers...and I absolutely renounce every custom and institution of the Jewish law."[1]

These customs the Gentile believers were renouncing had been placed by God into the Jewish culture in order to tell His story and His unfolding plan. It is such a shame that all those Christians were missing the richness of their heritage of being grafted into the olive tree of Israel and Judaism, and their rejection of the Jews' experience brought horrible results, both in the long term and short term.

EMPEROR CONSTANTINE BECOMES A CHRISTIAN

Constantine imposed Christianity upon the entire Roman Empire, in name at least. He said about the Jews though, "We desire to have nothing in common with the so-hated people. For the Redeemer has marked out another path for us. To this we will keep and be free from disgraceful association with these people."[1] With the Roman Empire being "Christian," the level of persecution against the Jews began to rise to a whole different level. Before, anti-Semitism was just directed locally or individually; now the whole government of Rome was against the Jew. And along came State-sanctioned persecution of the Jews. In 325, Constantine called together the Council of Nicea.

> Netzarim were excluded from the meeting. Jewish practices were banned. The "Day of the Sun" was substituted for the Biblical Sabbath. For the first time Gentile Christianity officially labeled the Nazarenes as apostates. From this time forward Nazarenes begin to be listed in the catalogs of apostate movements.[14]

JOHN CHRYSOSTOM, the Father of the Orthodox Church, known as "the preacher with the golden tongue" was one of the most popular and greatest orators of his time and beyond. He became the Bishop of Constantinople in the late 380's. He delivered a series of sermons against the Jews:

> The Jews are the most worthless of all men. They are lecherous greedy, rapacious. They are perfidious murderers of Christ. They worship the Devil. Their religion is a sickness. For killing God there is no expiation possible...Christians must never cease vengeance and Jews must live in servitude forever.

191

God always hated the Jews. It is incumbent upon all
the Christians to hate the Jews.[1]

After these sermons were delivered, Christians rushed out of churches
and started attacking synagogues!

What Bible was he reading? Chrysostom was a scholar who read the
Bible, he should have known better! It is inexcusable that he planted
such disgusting diatribes into the foundation of the Church for the
uneducated and illiterate masses to digest, with no recourse for
reading on their own the actual way God feels about the Jewish
people that is found even in the New Testament by writers such as the
Apostle Paul (Rabbi Sha'ul) in his letter to the Romans.

> **Romans 11:11-23.** I say then, have they stumbled that
> they should fall? Certainly not! But through their fall,
> to provoke them to jealousy, salvation *has come* to the
> Gentiles. [12] Now if their fall *is* riches for the world,
> and their failure riches for the Gentiles, how much
> more their fullness!
> [13] For I speak to you Gentiles; inasmuch as I am an
> apostle to the Gentiles, I magnify my ministry, [14] if by
> any means I may provoke to jealousy *those who are*
> my flesh and save some of them. [15] For if their being
> cast away *is* the reconciling of the world, what *will*
> their acceptance *be* but life from the dead?
> [16] For if the firstfruit *is* holy, the lump *is* also *holy;* and
> if the root *is* holy, so *are* the branches. [17] And if some
> of the branches were broken off, and you, being a wild
> olive tree, were grafted in among them, and with them
> became a partaker of the root and fatness of the olive
> tree, [18] do not boast against the branches. But if you do
> boast, *remember that* you do not support the root, but
> the root *supports* you.
> [19] You will say then, "Branches were broken off that I
> might be grafted in." [20] Well *said.* Because of unbelief
> they were broken off, and you stand by faith. Do not
> be haughty, but fear. [21] For if God did not spare the

natural branches, He may not spare you either. [22] Therefore consider the goodness and severity of God: on those who fell, severity; but toward you, goodness, if you continue in *His* goodness. Otherwise you also will be cut off. [23] And they also, if they do not continue in unbelief, will be grafted in, for God is able to graft them in again.

CHURCH FATHER EPIPHANIUS gave a description of the general Christian outlook on the Jewish believers of the time. "We shall now especially consider heretics who...call themselves Nazarenes; they are mainly Jews and nothing else. They make use not only of the New Testament, but they also use in a way the Old Testament of the Jews; for they do not forbid the books of the Law, the Prophets, and the Writings...They differ from the Jews because they believe in Messiah, and from the Christians in that they are to this day bound to the Jewish rites, such as circumcision, the Sabbath, and other ceremonies."[12; 14]

SAINT AUGUSTINE IN NORTH AFRICA AND JEROME OF ITALY (VULGATE WRITER) CORRESPOND. Jerome wrote a series of very negative things about the Jews especially the Netzarim around the 380's/400's. He called them compromisers because they kept some Jewish traditions and said they should relinquish all their Jewish identity when becoming Christians. Augustine wrote back to Jerome and said, "In the beginning the Jews should have been keeping the Torah as commanded by God as a 'transitional period'" but today he agreed with Jerome that they should not. Augustine did not encourage violence against the Jews as Jerome did though. Augustine said, "Leave the Jews alone as the

"Leave the Jews alone as the accursed people of the world so that the church will recognize what happens to people who reject Christ."
–Augustine

accursed people of the world so that the church will recognize what happens to people who reject Christ."

While that is not a great stance to take on God's chosen people, it is better than most of these major Christian Church fathers' views. Augustine's line of thinking prevailed over the Western Church's actions for about 600 years. Chrysostom's writings guided the Eastern Church.

What began as an offshoot of the Jewish faith created a religion that was wildly anti-Jewish. And it led to horrible persecution and destruction of property and life in the years to come. It is the Biblical principle of sowing and reaping. These hate-filled ideas were sown into "baby" Christianity and as the Church matured, the hate also grew and bore fruit, multiplied many times over, across the world.

These quotes of arrogant rejection I have laid out for you is how the majority of Jewry experienced Christianity, and this was just the beginning stages. While there has been a beautiful shift in the last 40 years especially in the western Evangelical Church toward supporting the Jewish people, as we discover our Jewish roots, it will take more than a few years to un-do all that has been done against the Jewish people.

PERSONAL CHALLENGE

There are many good things the church has contributed to the earth, but this part of history of the church is hard for true Christians to hear, much less digest and accept. I challenge you to pray and ask God to reveal any hidden or obvious place in your heart that has accepted any of the ideas of Replacement Theology or rejection of the Jews, then repent and renounce those lies of the enemy and accusations and condemnations made against the Jewish people. Ask for a fresh start and revelation of God's heart for the Jewish people, and a heart that would recognize Who our Root is. Ask God for reconciliation between Jews and Gentiles that the plan of God for one new man would come forth in the whole world.

את

GOD'S SENDS AN UNLIKELY SAVIOR
FOR THE JEWISH PEOPLE.

BYZANTINE EMPIRE

Justinian took over part of the Holy Roman Empire around 520-530 AD and formed a new empire called Byzantium. His land spread from the Balkans thru present-day Turkey and was called the Eastern Roman Empire. In 537 Justinian finished building the largest church in the world, called the *Hagia Sofia* in Constantinople. He was so awed by it, that he actually rode a horse into the church and fell off and cried out, "Solomon, I have surpassed you!"[1]

There were tremendous conflicts within the Church at that time, especially concerning the trinity and variations on the trinity. When ordinary people had simple theological disputes, they turned them into wars! The whole region was unstable under Justinian. He persecuted Christians who didn't agree with him on every theological issue. Jews, and lots of them, lived in his empire; they obviously didn't agree with him. They were persecuted and sometimes killed.

But God raised up an unlikely savior for the Jewish people. This man was in a pagan temple when he had a revelation of "the one true god," and he tried to convince his pagan neighbors about this god, but they rejected him. He left the area for another city and made the same proclamation. Those people accepted and adopted his ideology. Then he returned and forced the first city to surrender to him, and thus began the Islamic Empire. The person we are talking about is

Mohammad. Over the next 100 years, Islam swept the whole region into a new empire.

Really? Islam as a savior for the Jewish people? Yes. Historically, Islam has treated Jews much better than Christians did. It was only in the last 80 years or so that the relationship between Muslims and Jews has deteriorated. [That decline can be traced to one man: Haj Amin al Husseini, the Mufti of Jerusalem beginning in 1921. He had a vision for a pan-Arabic Empire (with himself as its leader, of course) with no place for anyone outside the Islamic faith. Especially Jews!]

There is evidence that the sect of the Netzarim remained viable until at least the thirteenth century.[14] Since the rebirth of the modern State of Israel in 1948, there has been a resurgence of Jews who believe in Jesus. They were around before, but not in the numbers they are now. Nearly every major city in Israel has a congregation of Messianic believers. Nearly every American city of significant size also has a congregation of Messianic believers.

What is particularly difficult for Messianic believers is that they are not fully accepted as "normal" by either side of the schism. The Jews think Messianics have thrown off their Jewishness, and thus God, because they believe Yeshua is God's son, the promised Messiah. Christians reject Messianics because they follow too many of the Torah laws set forth for them by God. Christians as a whole tend to think that if a person follows the law, he or she is rejecting the freedom Jesus died to give us. (So are they free *not* to follow the law, but not free *to* follow the Law? That doesn't make sense).

HERE IS MY TAKE: Messianic Believers have the best of both worlds and should be sought out for instruction concerning the depths of Christianity we are missing since the Church rejected the "first half" of Christianity when they rejected Christianity's Jewish heritage. At every opportunity we should encourage Messianic Jews to follow whichever laws God has laid on their consciences to follow.

There are a couple of different kinds of commands in the Torah. The positive and negative commands I am sure you are familiar with. But there are many commands where the Lord uses words such as "throughout your generations" or "forever, in all your generations." Those commands don't get cancelled out or done away with for Jews, whether they believe in Jesus or not. Because Jewish people are in Covenant with God by their blood, Jews are required to complete those commands. We should support them in their obedience! According to the writings of the New Testament the only requirements for Gentile Christians are the four in Luke 15 that all boil down to not participating in any idolatry.

> **Luke 15:28-29** For it seemed good to the Holy Spirit, and to us, to lay upon you no greater burden than these necessary things: [29] that you abstain from things offered to idols, from blood, from things strangled, and from sexual immorality.

As was appropriate, the Jewish church fathers of the New Testament seemed most concerned about making sure that Gentile believers were following the same God as they were being taught about, Yahweh, not some strange new god. These four items were commonly known as the worship rituals associated with false gods. Abstaining from these things was the best way for the Gentiles to show that they were clinging to the God of Abraham, Isaac and Jacob, only.

END NOTES

The primary information in this chapter, even the idea to study further in the Jewish split with Messianic Jews, came from Rabbi Jamie Cowan's fantastic Jewish History Seminar. I added additional resources as verification, but the ground work credit goes all to Rabbi Cowan's in depth research skills.

1. Cowan, Jamie Rabbi. Jewish History Seminar. Richmond (Virginia) International House of Prayer. Summer 2010.

2. Rich, Tracey R. (2011). Retrieved August 6, 2013 from http://www.jewfaq.org/gentiles.htm

3. Thaler, Valerie S. (n.d.) "Jewish attitudes toward proselytes." Retrieved August 7, 2013 from http://www.myjewishlearning.com/beliefs/Issues/Jews_and_Non-Jews/Attitudes_Toward_Non-Jews/Converts.shtml?p=2

4. Angel, Marc D. (2005). *Choosing to Be Jewish.* K'Tav Publishing. NY.

5. Time of Barnabas's writing. Retrieved August 7, 2013 from http://www.earlychristianwritings.com/barnabas.html

6. The Epistle of Barnabas. Retrieved August 7, 2013 from http://www.mb-soft.com/believe/txv/barnabas.htm

7. ben Friedman, Moreh. Yashanet.com retrieved August 8, 2013 from http://www.yashanet.com/library/nazarene_judaism.html

8. Lederer, Michael. July 17, 2012. *Debunking the myth that Messianic Jews abandoned the Jewish people in the Roman revolt by Dr Jeffery L. Seif.* Sar-Shalom-Plano.com. Retrieved August 8, 2013 from http://www.sarshalom-plano.com/_blog/Articles/post/Debunking_the_Myth_that_Messianic_Jews_Abandoned_the_Jewish_People_in_the_Roman_Revolt_by_Dr_Jeffrey_L_Seif/

9. Tertullian *Apology I* Translated by Rev. S. Thelwall, Late Scholar of Christ's College, Canterbury. Chapter XXI retrieved August 15, 2013 from http://www.biblestudytools.com/history/early-church-fathers/ante-nicene/vol-3-latin-christianity/tertullian/apology.html

10. Shoenburg, Shira. 2013. The Jewish Virtual Library. *The Bar-Kochba Revolt.* Published by The Israeli-American Cooperative Enterprise. Retrieved August 20, 2013 from http://www.jewishvirtuallibrary.org/jsource/Judaism/revolt1.html

11. Bar Kokba War. 1906. *Jewish Encyclopedia.* Retrieved August

21, 2013 from http://www.jewishencyclopedia.com/articles/2464-bar-cochba-bar-cochbah You can find the quote in paragraph 10.

12. (Epiphanius; Panarion 29; translated from the Greek).

13. Church father quotes compiled by Armstrong, Dave. 2008. Anti-Semitism in the Church fathers and historically among Catholics: Resources and recent Catholic "Institutional Repentance". Retrieved August 28, 2013 from http://www.catholicfidelity.com/anti-semitism-in-the-church-fathers-by-dave-armstrong/

14. Quote from ben Freidman, Moreh. Yahsnet.com retrieved August 29, 2013 from http://www.yashanet.com/library/nazarene_ judaism.html

15. Justin Martyr. (n.d.) Early Christian writings. Retrieved June 16, 2014 from http://www.earlychristianwritings.com/text/justinmartyr-dialoguetrypho.html

10

SELDOM TAUGHT STORIES OF
THE JEWS IN THE MIDDLE AGES

THE CRUSADES

After Islam came into Byzantium, the Muslims just kept sweeping in. In the late 1000's AD there was a radical Islamic group that came up out of Africa and into Spain creating trouble for the Jews. So the Jews began migrating. Some went into North Africa and Palestine, but others went to Northern Spain and France and up into Germany. There were small Jewish communities scattered in those regions already, but now a larger number of Jews were entering "Christian" Europe for the first time. At first they were welcomed in by the Christian groups because the Jews brought knowledge and prosperity gained by living in the Islamic Empire. At that time the Islamic Empire was far more advanced than the backward European nations who were just coming out of the Dark Ages. (Even though this is opposite of what we think today.)

Europe was made up of feudal societies during the late 1000's, in which the lord of the land owned a castle and all the surrounding land. The peasants farmed for him. The lords always looked for ways to expand their holdings, but they needed money to do that. The new Jews from Islamic lands in the east brought in the money and knowledge to do expand. These Jews were offered a "charter" that allowed them to live within their own communities, practice their own religion without persecution and live a decent life. They were not allowed to own land or practice the crafts to become silversmiths, blacksmiths, or shoemakers etc. However, they could trade and do money lending.

Money lending was key, because the Bible prescribed how it could be done, even among Christians. Both Christians and Jews were following the same doctrines God laid out in Leviticus 25 and Deuteronomy 23 for money lending. God says no interest is to be charged to a brother, but the foreigner or "heathen" is fair game. Well, the European lords were fresh out of cash when the Jews began to flock into their lands. The Jews brought money with them. Since the Jews considered Christian Europe "foreign" and the lords considered the Jews "heathens," they were both biblically sound in their loaning practices. The Jews loaned money to the lords who expanded their land holdings, and thus, Europe expanded.

ROOTS OF CHRISTIAN ANTI-SEMITISM[1]

However the roots of Christian anti-Semitism began to show growth. There are three main roots:

> **ETHNIC:** Until this point the Christians in Europe (Visigoths, Franks, and Germans) are the only ethnic groups. They all

202

look alike, speak the same language, have the same religion and same culture. They even dressed the same. All of a sudden the Jews came into town. They all wore black, spoke a different language, lived a different culture and promoted a different value system, and a different religion. Society was shaken, wondering, "who are these strange people?" Immigrants have always been treated with suspicion. Even now, in the U.S., the most welcoming nation to immigrants ever, we are skeptical of those who enter our country and are not likes us. Christian Europeans were scared that they would be changed by these strange Jews.

RELIGION: Not only is the Jewish religion different from Christianity, but the prevailing belief of the time was that the Jews killed the Christian God. At first, the Christians just wanted the Jews to believe the way they believed. But the Jews weren't interested. There were three factors that kept the Jews from being interested:

> TRINITY: Judaism is based on the notion that there is only *one* God. The Shma from Deuteronomy 6:4, the most famous Jewish prayer, reflects this, "Here oh Israel, the Lord our God, the Lord is one." And any way you present the Trinity, it looks like three, not one.

> "YOU'RE FREE FROM THE LAW." The problem with that Christian statement is that following the law is what makes a Jew a Jew. Christians expected Jews to give up this thing that God gave to them way back at Mount Sinai. And the statement is problematic anyway, because no genuine Christian really believes it. Consider the fuss U.S. Christians threw when the Ten Commandments were banned from schools and courthouses. If Christians are "free from the law,"

wouldn't it be fine to steal or kill? Well, no. Because we know it is wrong and would hurt our relationship with Jesus. But where does that "wrongness" come from? The Torah! For all the modern proponents of grace doctrine (yes, this is the age of grace, no dispute there) consider whether it is possible to have grace, if you have no law. It's not. The law is the standard from which we receive grace. Beyond that, even the Jews can see that the New Testament contains more stringent laws than the basic laws of the Old Testament. No murder versus do not be angry with your brother. This Christian incoherency doesn't make any sense to the Jews.

AESTHETICISM. Basically Christians ascribe to being removed from "this world." Christians are not to participate in worldly activities. Holiness, righteousness, and piety were equated with being poor (Thanks, Saint Francis of Assisi). But the Jews love to party and have a good time; they are blessed to make money. Their faith emphasizes having an enjoyment of *this life*, where Christianity focuses on the afterlife.

Messianic Rabbi Jamie Cowan says, "With this deal of Christianity, the Jews would have to reject who they are *and* live a bummed out life. No wonder they said no thanks!"[1]

ECONOMICS: The final root of anti-Semitism is economics. Money is often the final straw. The Jews couldn't own land, they couldn't work the crafts, but they could lend money. To earn a living, the Jews had to charge interest, and were perfectly right in doing so. The lords decided they needed *more* money, so they started to tax the Jews on their profits.

But when the middle man gets taxed, what does he do? He raises interest rates. Since the peasants were also borrowing money from the Jews to help them get through different situations or difficult circumstances, they also were charged the higher rates, but they couldn't see that it was the lords who had increased the taxes causing the higher interest rates. The peasants became even more impoverished. It looked to them like the Jews were stealing all their money. This set up a scenario that was a potential disaster for the Jews. They were between the lords and the masses; they already looked different and had a different religion; they acted differently too. The only necessity was a spark.

THE SPARK OCCURRED IN 1094-1095

From the 600's to the 1090's Byzantium (now Turkey) remained sovereign, but the Islamic empire had been taking over more and more of the Middle East and moving into the west. In 1054, there was a church split. The western and eastern churches officially split. Eastern Orthodoxy ruled people out of Constantinople in Byzantium, and Roman Catholicism ruled people from Rome.

In 1094, Constantinople called on the pope to help combat incursions by the Islamic Empire in his region. Pope Urban, in 1095, issued a decree to all the churches under him (the whole west) to raise up an army to "liberate Jerusalem." What did that have to do with defending Byzantium? Nothing. Urban probably didn't think rescuing Eastern Orthodoxy was a good enough reason, so his idea was to raise this army with Jerusalem as its PR (public relations) point. He would stop by Byzantium to help them out on the way to the Holy Land. It was a crusade to take Jerusalem back from the Infidels!

To offer a short version of the Pope's crazy scripture-twisting reasoning, he felt it was okay to kill and go to war with people as long as they were not Christian. This became a serious problem for the Jews. As the Christians rose up in an army and sewed big crosses on their clothing to go fight the infidels, they suddenly realized they had been infiltrated years earlier and had infidels within their midst. The Jews. On their way out of town, the Crusaders began killing the Jews who lived among them.

IN 1096, THE FIRST CRUSADE BEGAN. NINE CRUSADES WILL FOLLOW

Wherever Jews were found as the Crusaders moved east through Europe, they began to slaughter entire communities. It started in Worms, Germany and continued all the way to Constantinople and then into Jerusalem. Thousands and thousands died. Some were given the option to convert if they wanted, or they were murdered. About this time, Rabbi Rashi, who is considered the greatest Talmudic commentator of all time and the owner of a vineyard in France, issued a decree to the Jews called *Kiddush HaShem* or "Sanctification of the name." It said the Jews could commit suicide, for the sake of the divine Name of Go, if the choice they are forced into is sure death at the hand of the Crusaders or forced conversion through torture. In York during the 3rd Crusade (led by Richard the Lionhearted) all the Jews committed suicide to avoid being forcibly converted. It happened at various other times and places as well.

Along the route, Crusaders mistook some fellow Christians for Jews and tortured, gutted and burned them alive too. When the Crusaders arrived in Jerusalem, it was a multi-cultural city where the Jews, Christians and Muslims were getting along famously. Apparently no one told the pope that the Christians didn't need help. However, July 8, 1099, the Crusaders attacked and breeched the wall of Jerusalem. They took captive all the Jews, and threw them into the great synagogue and burned it down, with the Jews still alive inside. The

Crusaders paraded around outside singing "Christ is worthy, the Lamb is worthy, Christ the son of God" while the Jews burned alive.[1] The following day, the Crusaders did the same thing to the Muslims. Rounded them up and threw them in a mosque and burned it down. It is no wonder that Jews are not interested in Christianity.

את

POST CRUSADE ERA

Nine more crusades followed the first. The Crusades are difficult to understand, but Christianity had been invaded by an idea that war and valor were part of Christianity's value.[1] In the early 1900's we experienced the healing movement, today we have the prayer and worship movement, but then, they had war and valor movement. It must have started as a kind of a "Jesus the conquering King" idea of being Christ-like. But it got very twisted.

These gruesome times altered Augustine's caution that Christians had lived by for centuries: Leave the Jews alone as the example of God's accursed people. (Not that Augustine's is right either!) Consequently, anti-Semitic violence invaded the church and consumed it for the next 500 years. Wild accusations began and continued; the same things kept happening over and over again, these are the three things:

#1 BLOOD LIBEL: the idea that Jews take the blood of Christians, especially Christian children and mix it with the making of their unleavened bread. These accusations caused outbreaks of tremendous persecution wherever Jews lived. Persecution included synagogues being burned down or whole communities being slaughtered.

#2 RITUAL MURDER CHARGE: started in Norwich, England in 1144. A young boy, a tanner's apprentice went missing near Easter time. Some maids said they saw the boy enter some Jewish homes in the city. So there was an investigation, and suddenly this boy was found dead in the forest with stab wounds. The investigators went to the Jewish homes and tortured the Jews until they admitted they stabbed this boy as a ritual murder to reenact the death of Christ before Easter. It was a complete fabrication, but as a result of this lie thousands more Jews were slaughtered in Norwich. Then the ritual murder charges resounded across Europe for centuries. Even as recently as 70-80 years ago, this came up in Hungary, Yugoslavia, Kiev and Belarus. Currently, Muslims have begun to reproduce this centuries-old lie against the Jews.

#3 DESECRATION OF THE HOST: In 1215, the Laturn Council ruled that the bread of communion was the actual body of Christ (called transubstantiation). Shortly, the Jews were accused of bribing Christians into handing over their communion wafers, then taking the wafers and stabbing them so that they could kill Jesus over and over again (because He could *feel* the stabbings). In 1298, in Ratingen, Germany/Rhineland some Christians even claimed they witnessed a miraculous "bleeding of the host." (Interesting.) The entire population of Jews in Ratingen was burned alive! Then 140 other communities were slaughtered; about 100,000 Jews were killed in six months of persecution based on this one lie.

LATURN COUNCIL OF 1215

The main goal for the Laturn Council meeting was to unify Church leaders' beliefs. There was some concern about some heretical groups that had sprung up in the Church from strange thinking the Crusaders brought back from their "time abroad" in the east. At this time good groups such as the Cathorists and Waldonesians (pre-John Huss reformers) were spreading their truth and lifestyles very well.

So the Church representatives formed a group of special monks called the Dominican Order. The Order's mission was to investigate and root out heresy wherever they found it. One tactic they used was to go into towns, do an inquisition and torture the people to find the leaders and try them, and then burn them at the stake. However the church leaders and inquisitors were also concerned about Jews infecting and influencing Christianity. Their goal was to purify the Church. So Jews within their midst were required to wear special clothing with a yellow marker on them (hmmm, sounds familiar!) so the people would know not to listen to them.[1] This was the first time the Jews were targeted and isolated in this way.

DISPUTATIONS. The Church was also interested in challenging and converting the Jews to Christianity, so they held public debates called disputations. They forced leading rabbis to publicly debate their faith against Jewish converts, and the debates would last a couple of weeks at a time. Then, while the rabbis were away from their congregations, the Dominicans, or Christian groups would go in to the rabbi's Jewish communities and forcibly convert them or burn down their synagogue. The 1263 Disputation of Barcelona was the most famous disputation. The Christian leaders' use of converted Jews in disputations is a major reason that Messianic Jews have been so hated by the regular Jewish community.

EXPULSION. Well, when the Church couldn't kill them all and couldn't convert them all, the next logical step was to kick them out of their nations.

ENGLAND: Jews kicked were out in 1290, and all Jewish were assets seized.

FRANCE: In the early 1300's, 100,000 Jews were told they must leave all goods and debts owed them behind, and they were given one month to leave. All jewelry and money was confiscated by Crown.

France's motivation was robbery; the king's funds had been depleted by war.

PASSION PLAYS[1]

The Passion Plays were instrumental in this crazy thinking throughout Europe. Christians would reenact Jesus' last week on earth on stage near Easter time. The Jews were portrayed as devils through costumes and stage make-up. The producers used "modern" Middle-Ages Jewish names for the characters, and it incited violence and ill-will among the populations wherever these plays were performed. It was a miserable time for Jewish people.

SPAIN: In 1248, Christians retook Spain from the Muslims. Jewish life in Spain had been pretty good for many, many years under the Muslims. When persecutions and burnings were going on elsewhere in Europe, the Spanish Jews were doing well. Even after Christians came in, the Jews were used as a transitional force between Christians and Muslims. They helped govern the region, but things begin to change with the Bubonic Plague; it was blamed on the Jews.

Then in 1390, two leaders in Castile, Spain died and the Jews were blamed. A horrible pogrom broke out on June 4, 1391. One hundred thousand Jews were murdered, one hundred thousand Jews converted to Christianity, and one hundred thousand emmigrated from Spain. The Jews were used to getting kicked out of places, but the thing that shocked the Jews the most was that so many Jews converted. So the Jewish leaders began to examine their huge erosion of faith. In 1414, there was another mass conversion to Christianity in Spain. Fifty thousand more left Judaism for Christianity. At the same time there was an increased fervor in Messianic expectation—for both Christians and Jews—because in 1453, the *Hagia Sofia*, the massive Christian Church built by Constantine, in Constantinople, was taken by the

JEWS IN THE MIDDLE AGES

Ottoman Turks, the Muslims. (Even today, the church is a mosque.) The people just didn't think it could get worse than that. Their cry was "the end of time is upon us!" [1]

THREE GROUPS OF JEWS IN SPAIN

The three categories of Jews who lived in Spain were regular Jews, Conversos, and a sub category of Conversos called Moranos. The Moranos were secretly Jews but outwardly Christians. After Jews converted to Christianity, there was no limit to what they could do or attain in Spanish society. Even nobility! So, it became very attractive for the Jewish people to convert. Pressure increased throughout Spanish society, because there was more competition for good jobs and higher societal positions, because nothing was withheld from the converts. Then in the 1460's a law was passed differentiating between the "new" and "old" Christians. New Christians were no longer eligible for the better positions. So Jewishness was no longer a religious difference—they were both Christians—it became a *race* problem. This will come up again in Holocaust.

The Conversos became isolated. If they reverted back to Judaism, they would be persecuted or killed. Then they became extremely isolated with the institution of the Inquisition!

INQUISITION

So it begins. In 1469, Ferdinand from Aragon married Isabella from Castile to unite the kingdoms in all of Spain, though Granada in the south was still held by Muslims. The Jews actually supported the marriage, because Ferdinand's grandfather was a Jew, and they had been well treated by his family. The Jews assumed the pressure they were under would diminish under Ferdinand's leadership. In 1479, the kingdoms merged into Spain. But in 1478, the year before, the Pope had made a decree: examine the genuineness of Jewish conversions in Castile. The church leaders were concerned that people were converting for the wrong reasons. Well, of *course* they were!

In 1481, the pope established the Office of the Inquisitor General in Spain. The Grand Inquisitor's name was Torquemada, and he was from the Dominican Order! The Inquisitor General's goal was not to target the Jews, but the Conversos, to ensure Christianity was pure and conversions were made for genuine purposes.[1] Inquisitors would set up courts of inquiry in different cities and began to investigate. They would torture anyone who *appeared* guilty to find converts who were keeping the Jewish traditions. The investigators would try to trick the converts, such as in the market, by having people offer pork products to Conversos to see if they would take them. If they refused the product, they were suspected of keeping Jewish traditions. The inquisitor would then arrest the Converso and torture him/her to find more false converts. Another tactic was entering the Jewish communities on Friday nights, to peek in the windows looking for people lighting candles for Shabbat. The Jews all lived in one community at this time, the Jews, Conversos and Moranos together.

Thousands of Jews, mainly Conversos and Moranos, were executed at the stake. There were public confessions and burnings. The Jews were required to wear special clothes, and suffered horrible torture such as the rack. Church inquisitors even used knives under toenails to make sure these people were not keeping Jewish tradition.

In 1491 there was a Blood Libel in Toledo, Spain. Under torture, people named several Conversos *and* Jews that were involved in this blood libel and in a plot to overthrow Christianity. Suddenly, this became a turning point to expel *all* Jews out of Spain.

On January 2, 1492, the Spanish conquered Granada and unified all Spain "under the banner of Christ" with one exception, the Jews. The

Jews were the only non-Christian group left. So Ferdinand issued an order on March 31 that same year. The edict said the Jews had four months to get out of Spain or convert to Christianity; there were hundreds of thousands of Jews. If they left, they could take no gold, silver or any other form of wealth with them, and they were not allowed to sell their possessions or businesses anyway. The Jews were frantic about what to do. No country wanted them. Finally, they raised millions and millions of dollars in today's standard, and gave it to King Ferdinand's treasurer, Don Isaac Abravanel, who happened to be a Jew and a personal friend to the king. The Jews said, "Take this money and try to persuade the king to change his mind, and let us stay."[1]

ABRAVENEL

When Abravanel approached the king, Torquemada (Inquisitor General) heard he was going and intervened by arriving first. Torquemada addressed the king in front of the court and basically called him a Judas if he "sells Jesus" for the money the Jews were willing to give him. "I will take no blame. You are responsible to God for this business deal!" Torquemada said, and laid down a cross in front of the king and left.

Abravanel was watching the whole exchange. After Torquemada's challenge in front of so many witnesses, King Ferdinand could not have changed the decree even if he had wanted to. Ferdinand did offer to protect his friend Abravanel, but he would not "sell his soul" to save the Jews. Abravanel chose to go with his own people.

9TH OF AV

So many bad things have happened to the Jews on the 9th of Av that it is a national day of mourning.

1. Israel chose to believe the spies' bad report in the desert.
2. Solomon's Temple fell, 586 BC
3. 2nd temple sacked, 70 AD
4. Jerusalem plowed, 130 AD
5. Fall of Betar, 133 AD
6. Expelled from England, 1290
7. Spanish Inquisition, 1492
8. Vienna Expulsion, 1670
9. World War I, 1914
10. Final Solution announced, 1490
11. Warsaw Ghetto deportation, 1942
12. Gush Katif, Israel residents forced out by IDF & world pressure, 2006

Portugal eventually agreed to accept 120,000 Jews for eight months while they made arrangements to move on further. In August 1492, it turned out that the four-month deadline for them to leave Spain fell on the Hebrew calendar date of the 9th of Av. Two hundred thousand Jews left; one hundred thousand more converted. As soon as the Jews arrived in Portugal, the king rescinded his agreement. He said, "Your choice is to convert to Christianity or you'll be turned over as slaves."

Then the king of Portugal ordered the Jewish children to be taken from their parents; the soldiers literally took them out of their parents' arms! He sent the children via ship to a newly discovered island off Africa, Sao Tome', which was inhabited by lizards, snakes and other beasts. The mothers were not allowed to go.

One mother actually threw herself into the sea with her two-year-old child from the gangplank.[1] Most people couldn't swim, and she was one of them. Both mother and child drowned.

Where was the Lord? It had been hundreds of years of torment. The Lord's people kept getting kicked out of their homes and countries or

214

murdered or forced to convert. This is where the idea of the wandering Jew came from. But the Lord was working secretly behind the scenes to raise up a "savior" from an unlikely source.

CHRISTOPHER OF COLOGNE

In the late 1400's there was an adventurous young man who lived in the port town of Cologne, Italy, which happened to be a Jewish town. He wanted to explore the world so in 1484, he moved to Spain, because Spain was a major seafaring nation. He quickly kept company with both Jews and Muslims, but especially Conversos.[1] We know this young man by the name Christopher Columbus.

He thought he could get to India via the Atlantic Ocean, which of course is not accurate. But it doesn't matter. What's interesting about Columbus is that it is likely that he was a Converso himself. Here's why[1]:

- His last name was Colon which is a Jewish family name
- Most of his friends were Conversos or other Jews
- When dating all of his correspondence he used the date from the destruction of the second temple; not the birth of Christ. So everything was 70 years less than what most people were using at this time. For example, instead of 1485 he would have used 1405.
- At the end of letters that he wrote to his son, he added a cipher for the Hebrew abbreviation for "B'ezra Ha Shem," which means in English "With the help of God"
- He showed strong interest in Jewish matters in Spain and Italy.
- In his correspondence from the West, he included many references to the Hebrew scriptures, which was basically unknown at this time in Christianity.

- He took six identifiable Conversos aboard his three ships, *Nina, Pinta* and *Santa Maria* to the West.
- He spoke Hebrew; his cartographer was Jewish and all the notes the two of them made on their maps and charts were in Hebrew.[2]
- His original plan was to leave on the 2nd of August—on the Hebrew calendar the 9th of Av—he decided to postpone the sailing until that evening after sundown so that he wouldn't be associated with that date. He was probably familiar with the Jewish teaching that any work performed on the 9th of Av would come to no good.[3] Like any good Jew knows, sundown marks the beginning of the new day. So he actually sailed on the 10th of Av.

Some interesting things happened on board Columbus' ships. He sailed south to the Canary Islands on the West African coast to resupply before heading west. After departing there on September 6, 1492,[5] Columbus remarked in one of his writings that one particular evening he heard a weird chanting on one of the ships, then suddenly it sprang up on the other ships as well.

By this time fall had crept up on the crew, and Columbus identified the sound as being the beginning of the Hebrew prayer that is prayed only on Yom Kippur, the Day of Atonement. This prayer is called the *Kol Nedray*, which means "all vows." The *Kol Nedray* is an ancient Jewish prayer that had become much more important in the previous hundred years of persecution. The tradition calls for Jews, at the beginning of Yom Kippur, to renounce all vows that they made unwittingly during the previous year. It was a way that the Conversos could show God and each other that they were still Jewish and honoring the Covenant God of their people even if they had gone through a forced conversion. They wanted to reconnect to the God of Israel.

So Columbus heard and identified this prayer by the Conversos on his crew as they traveled across the ocean on Yom Kippur.

Later, another interesting story[1] came from Columbus's Chief Lieutenant, who was one of the six Conversos sailing with Columbus. Late in September 1492, the lieutenant saw something floating in the water. He fished it out and it was a palm branch. After thinking for a moment he suddenly realized that it was the Festival of *Hoshana Raba*, the last day of the Feast of Tabernacles. The day the Jews are supposed to take palm branches and wave them before the Lord and to say "Save us, save us, save us, Oh God!" and this branch had come from the New World, from near the islands like Jamaica. It was floating in the water, almost as if to greet them. The beauty of this story is that the New World became the salvation of the Jewish people.[1]

Even before World War II when the Americans finally jumped in and saved the European Jews from being completely wiped out, many Jews had immigrated to the U.S. in the 1600s, 1700s, 1800s, and 1900s.

So Columbus, a Jewish Christian, paved a way for salvation of the Jewish people, in the future, because he had a heart for his own heritage. Even though he didn't know he was going the wrong way, God said, "I can use that!" God can use us too when we keep our hearts in tune with Him, even if we mess things up or act on a false premise like trying to get to India by sailing west.

After the Jews were expelled from Spain in 1492, they ended up being kicked out of Portugal too. Some went to Brazil or Holland, large numbers moved back east into the Ottoman Empire, especially in the southern Ottoman Empire in the Balkan States, which became Poland and Russia (most important group to keep a watch on). Others moved to North Africa, Italy and even Israel itself. This immigration is the first major group to return to the Promised Land during the second Diaspora. However, the Jews were still constantly moving within these regions and to different regions. Because such large groups of them were wandering (200,000+ people), the new regions would receive them at first, but would later kick them out because there were just too many Jews. Host nations felt like their resources were being overwhelmed and not available for their own people.

THE ITALY GROUP that migrated began working in the shipbuilding and iron industries there. Then the Italians began to react to the influx of the number of Jews by rioting. The authorities ended up building little walls around the Jewish settlements in the cities to protect them from the riots. The walled communities started being called "ghettos," which came from the Italian name for an iron foundry, *ghato*. The walled communities in Florence and Venice still have signage calling the developments *Ghato*. It was designed by the Italian government as a safety measure for the Jewish people. Unfortunately later in history the word *ghetto* took on a whole different meaning and function.

ELSEWHERE IN EUROPE THE RENAISSANCE sprang up with the development of the printing press. Humanism began to increase all over Europe, but it actually helped the Jews, because humanism diverted the people's focus from religion.

THE PROTESTANT REFORMATION which began in 1517 was not only a blessing to the Church, offering a transformation in the way people related to God, but it also helped the Jews because it basically split their enemy in two. The Christians began fighting each other, taking the heat off the Jews.

Martin Luther started off really well with the Jews, but when they didn't accept his gospel, he became increasingly anti-Semitic, and by the end of his life he wrote a pamphlet called "About the Jews and their Lies." In it, Luther called the Jews the accursed people. He suggested that Christians burn synagogues and bury anything that wouldn't burn so that there would be no remnant left for anyone to see. He wanted the Jews uprooted and their homes destroyed, so they would know they were exiles and accursed. He suggested, "Let's expel them forever."

The influence of Luther's writings did not end at his death. Combined with other anti-Semitic writings, Luther's writings became the foundation that Hitler used in the 1930's to justify what he was doing to the Jews.

IN 1618, THE THIRTY YEARS WAR broke out between Catholics and Protestants in Europe. The Jews were moneylenders and their lending was probably what extended the war to its extreme length. It was the profits from lending money to the peasants that gave the Jews the capital to lend to the leadership on both sides of the war. The prolonging of the war sent the peasants even deeper into debt and brought about intense resentment toward the Jews. In 1648, a group of Ukrainian peasants joined with the Khazak peasants and others and rose up in rebellion against the Catholics of Poland to break the bondage of the taxation. The rebels wanted to get at the source of the taxation which, in their eyes, was the Jews because of the money lending.

The Polish government protected the Jews at first, but eventually they allowed the rebels to have at the Jews in a massacre beyond massacres! Victims were filleted alive and infants were thrown into wells and buried alive.[1] The rebels removed Torah scrolls from synagogues and danced on them with whiskey. Even the slightest mercy toward a Jew was looked upon as treason. Only 1/10th of the Jewish population survived. Poland had been one of the most populous Jewish areas in the world. Until Hitler, this rebel peasant group under the leadership of Chimielnitchski was responsible for the greatest massacre of Jewish life.[4] The currency of Ukraine still carries Chimielnitchski's picture!

ENGLAND AGAIN. With the mess going on in Europe, Messianic fervor was stirred up again among the Jews *and* among the Christians, because it was nearly 1666. Oliver Cromwell and the Puritans were in a Messianic frame of mind and searched for Jesus' return in the years leading up to the dreaded 1666. People are all alike, looking for significance in a year number on a calendar, (which incidentally, is not God's calendar, so the year numbers are off anyway). The Christians and Jews were actually influencing each other about what they believed. The messiah was expected to appear, and so "he" did: May 31, 1665, in Gaza. His name was Shabbati Zvi.

He was kind of crazy, maybe bipolar. After some "good press" and performing some miracles, Zvi announced that he would present himself to the Sultan of the Ottoman Empire in Istanbul and demand that Israel be given back to the Jews. He asked the Jewish people all over the continent to pray and fast so it would happen. Riots broke out. The Sultan put Zvi in chains as soon as he arrived. While Zvi was imprisoned, the Sultan gave him an option to convert to Islam or be killed. Zvi converted. Then the ruse was up; Zvi was not the Messiah! The Jews were crushed in spirit, because it had seemed as if the end of all their suffering was at hand. Things had been so terrible for so long and then their messiah figure showed up, and they put their hope it him. But then it wasn't him.

את

GOD WORKS IN QUIET WAYS TO SAVE HIS PEOPLE

Even with all the suffering going on generation after generation, once again, God was working behind the scenes in a quieter way. This time it was a man in the Netherlands named Manasseh ben Israel.

Around 1650, ben Israel was studying the scriptures and searching for a resolve to the east/west Jewish problems. He saw that the west was changing and modernizing, and he wondered if they might accept the Jews now. As he studied the scriptures he came across a passage that said the Messiah will come when the Jews spread to the end of the earth. The same word used for "end" in Hebrew is the same word used for the nation of England.

Officially, the Jews had not been allowed in England since 1290, so ben Israel wrote a pamphlet called "Hope for Israel." He postulated that if the Jews were allowed into England that the Messiah would come. He decided to present this to the English leadership, who at this time in English history were particularly open to his idea. The Puritan movement had begun and was prevalent in the leadership. Oliver Cromwell and the Puritan commonwealth were in charge. One of the things the Puritans were known for was being millennialists, or experts on the second coming of Christ. They were actually one of the first groups ever to be pro-Jewish. They had already been writing about the Jews for 80 years when ben Israel wrote his pamphlet. Ben Israel met with Cromwell and showed him the prophecy. He told Cromwell, if the Jews are welcomed back into England, it could fulfill the prophecy and bring about the return of the messiah.

Cromwell went to Parliament and argued to rescind the 1290 law that barred Jews from living in England. It took two to three years of debate, but England's leadership recognized that Conversos had been living in England for the last 300 years anyway. So they decided to see what would happen, and Parliament allowed the non-converted Jews to come back in.

So, the Jews were welcomed back to England in the 1600's due to ben Israel's good salesmanship.

Why is this significant? Because from the 1580's to the 1900's it was England that helped the Jewish people return to Israel. England forced the hand of the world, and the Christians in England were actually working toward this even before the Jews were involved.

END NOTES

1. Cowen, Jamie. 2011. The Jewish History Seminar. Richmond VA, RIHOP.

2. *Jewish Roots of Christopher Columbus* video retrieved August 29, 2013 from http://www.youtube.com/watch?v=6hEyBSUv4EA

3. Harary, Albert. 2011. *The Jewish Forum*. Was Christopher Columbus Jewish Part 2 video retrieved August 29, 2013 from http://www.youtube.com/watch?v=NkXlEINS3m4

4. Chimeilnitchski information compiled October 18, 2013 from http://www.geschichteinchronologie.ch/eu/ukraine/EncJud_chmielnicki-pogroms-1648-1650-ENGL.html

5. Christopher Columbus Discovers America, 1492," EyeWitness to History, www.eyewitnesstohistory.com (2004). Retrieved January 23, 2014 from http://www.eyewitnesstohistory.com/columbus.htm

11

BACKGROUND ON THE HOLOCAUST

UNDERLYING PHILOSOPHY THAT LED TO THE HOLOCAUST

People often wonder, "How could an evil as deep and systematic as the Holocaust have occurred, especially to the most educated nation on the earth?"

We saw when we looked at the Middle Ages how the church viewed the Jews as being inhuman (the passion plays, the blood libels and the torture). People had to consider the Jews demonic in order for the church to accept these bizarre attacks against them and participate in the destruction of the Jews. There is no passion like that of religion, either true or false religion! But how could a country as highly educated as Germany come to a thought process that so thoroughly destroys human life, without any conscience?

It was a gradual process, like a frog in heating water, which started with the Protestant Reformation in the 16th century. During the Reformation, the societies of Western Europe were changing based on a new philosophy. It was a God-based philosophy that tried to establish a new society with God at the center. Lutherans, Puritans, Anabaptists, and Moravians were all reformers and movements that led to a change in society. These changes altered the politics of the 1700's. There was a move toward human rights on the political scene, and writers such as John Locke and Thomas Jefferson popped up. Unfortunately, with the rise in human rights awareness, people began to move away from the understanding of God-centeredness in society toward a man-centeredness. The focus on serving God waned and Western society got caught up with "worshipping" the new idea of human rights, rather than the One who revealed the change in society that needed to happen.

By the 1800's a whole new crop of philosophers had spilled into society; they spouted about humanity separate and apart from God. Men such as Hegel, Russo, Hume, and Hobbs. Hegel from Germany came up with a theory on how history moves forward. Hegelian Theory: You have a thesis (what exists), counter balanced by an anti-thesis (what "ideally" could exist) and when they clash, they bring about the best of all worlds. The combination or outcome of the two theses is called synthesis. Then the synthesis becomes "normal" or the new "thesis." Hegel assumed that the outcome or compromise of the two conflicting theories was *always* better than either of the two original theses.

As Hegel studied human history he applied his philosophical theory of life to it. He theorized if there was an existing body of society, then

224

a revolution or "response" to this society, would lead to a better society. Hegel looked at all of human history this way, and he wrote about it. Take a monarchy for example; the antithesis of monarchy is "anarchy" as represented by revolution (both American and French Revolutions had just taken place at the time Hegel was writing). So the synthesis in the new political system would be some form of democracy. It's not bad; there is some truth in this theory, but the thing is that synthesis is not always better; it is just different. However, deeper than that, this new (synthesis) form of government, democracy removes something from human history…God! God is not involved in this idea of democracy. It is rule by the majority, not by God. We have come fully away from what God is setting up, which is a Kingdom where He is King. Theocracy is His ultimate plan, though it really scares us to think of that right now, because of religious fanaticism worldwide whenever this is tried (i.e. Catholicism of the Middle Ages and current day Islam). But the last time, it is going to work! Yeshua will reign from Jerusalem where we will crown Him King and the nations will come each year at the Feast of Tabernacles, and at other times to worship Him there for 1,000 years. Not only will it be great, it will be perfect. Exactly as He planned from the beginning!

MARXISM

In the early to mid-1800's an economist, Karl Marx, picked up Hegel's idea (thesis + antithesis = synthesis) and applied it to form a new kind of economics. At this time the Industrial Revolution was creating havoc in European economics. Society change looked like this: Agricultural Society + Industrial Revolution = Capitalism. But it did not stop there. Marx saw gross inequities in capitalism; this new thesis of capitalism was normal when he was born, and he wanted to see a change in it. So when Marx saw capitalism as the thesis, his antithesis was the "rise of the industrial workers." It became the next revolution which then overthrew unregulated capitalism. It led to the synthesis of socialism. The great promise of socialism is equality and "everybody is happy." (Except happiness is never the outcome of socialism.)

In this same timeframe, Charles Darwin took Hegelian theory and applied it to biology. He called his theory "evolution." Darwin's theory took a particular species of animal as its thesis. He saw something happening to that species, like a radical climate change or a stronger predator, as the antithesis. The clash led to evolution of a new and better species, or "Survival of the Fittest."

The problem with Marx's idea is that socialism is a wonderful *concept*: everyone being equal. It sounds so good and noble. Everyone paying their "fair share," healthcare for everyone, no one goes hungry. But it only works in concept form. In socialism's equality, everyone quickly learns that it doesn't matter if they give their best, so they do not participate to their full potential. Socialism undermines God's principle of "if you don't work you don't eat," and it even steals people's desire and ability to give to others. (Based on this thought process: if the government takes my money to give to other people, then I don't need to give to others, and I don't have enough to give anyway.) Socialism tears down the human spirit of ingenuity, independence and hard work, personal responsibility and decision-making, and accountability to your fellow man and to God. But the *real* problem with Marx is that he doesn't figure God into socialism. He is an atheist. He says, "Religion is the opiate of the people." Therefore Marx's socialism removes God from economics.

The Hegelian theory removed God from history, from economics and from creation. So when society became steeped in this way of thinking, human life was no longer a reflection of God; human life became simply an evolved form. That's the crux of Darwinism. Unfortunately Darwinism is deeply engrained in our culture. There is a basic false premise way back at Hegelian Theory's conception: the compromise of two wrongs does not always bring about better, it just brings about different.

All patterns of thinking changed in the 1800's, and the intellectual world was absolutely captivated by it. Even the seminaries were affected. German seminaries were the best in the world. The greatest intellectuals and scholars all went there to study. Once Hegel's concepts became common ways to study life, it led to examining the Bible in the same manner.

Instead of seeing the Bible as being God's words divinely inspired, the Bible became the thesis. The early biblical characters became a primitive form of human understanding. (Israel was actually polytheistic until the prophets' timeframe. They believed that God was just the greatest among the gods. Prophets understood God differently: that there is only one God and all others are false.) Theologians being trained in the 1800's under Hegel Theory's influence then saw the changes in Israel's history as the antithesis, and Jesus became the "evolved form" of religion. The "better" of what came before. So it looked like Israel was "evolving," reinforcing the rightness of the theory to society. Really these biblical changes are just increased revelation, but when viewed through this worldview, it looked like evolving. And that was just the prophets, but when we get to Jesus, religion evolved even more. Jesus was now the loving God, where before we had the vengeful God of the Old Testament.

In line with the thinking of Hegelian theory, the *divinity* of the Bible was removed from the seminaries. The application of these principles to the Bible is called "higher criticism." Higher criticism subjected the Bible to critical theories about its origin just like any other piece of literature would be examined. So the biblical foundations of society became challenged in the seminaries. This still happens in seminaries today. Unfortunately, it became the modern and progressive and scientific way of thinking.

This change in thinking became hugely important because Hitler was *democratically* elected…because if Christians in Germany had stood by the principles of the Bible, he never would have been elected! He would have been cast off as a czar-maniac! But all of the underpinnings of society had eroded away through higher criticism, so everything else that Hitler argued for was attractive to a society that had just been shamed in WWI and hit with a huge war reparations bill. The people did not have the wherewithal to see through Hitler's raving, because they had been contaminated by Hegelian teaching. We will see how much Darwinism plays into German thought at the time Hitler comes to power.

There was one shining little lamp at this time, named Brown. He wrote a book warning people not to buy into these kinds of theories. He argued for a literal interpretation of scripture that God will restore literal Israel to physical Israel. He prevailed in Britain for a time, but outside Britain he had no influence.

HEGELIAN THEORY IN 19TH CENTURY EASTERN EUROPE AND GERMANY

There were wide chasms between social classes and poverty levels in Europe in the 19th century. But in Russia, Jewish rights just had been recognized for the first time. So there was a great irony throughout the world: Some Jews had become very wealthy and were helping finance the industrialization of society, but there was a stereotype floating around of Jews being at the forefront of revolution, throwing out the old order, and so forth. Crazily enough, the Jews were being criticized of both leading the hate of the societal changes *and* financing the revolutions.

The concept of "Jewish conspiracy" was left over from the blood libels centuries before. The rumors of ritual murders rose up again and shifted to an idea of a conspiracy that the Jews were planning to overthrow the World Order. Then a book that had been written in the late 1800's, *The Protocol of the Elders of Zion,* was twisted by an anti-Semite who accused the Jews of trying to overthrow the world. Then the Russian revolution began. Lots of Jews in Russia supported this revolution because it provided equal rights for them, for the first time in forever. From the outside, now it *looked* like the Jewish overthrow of the world was beginning through this communist revolution.

Back in Germany before WWI, Germans were the most educated society in the world. There was a great deal of pride in Germany and German culture. The Jews loved being German. Pre-WWI Germany was a very lawful nation; there was no civil violence at all. But after the war, all the killing and disorder had been such a shock, that the moral and civil order of Germany completely broke down. It became a lawless state. Latent anti-Semitism bubbled to the surface.

Two important writings influenced the German people, especially Hitler. One, Baron Gobenal's, *Essay of the Inequality of Mankind.* In it, he divided humans into categories. He took Darwinism and applied it to humans. Gobenal said the males with the strongest characteristics will find the females with the strongest characteristics to carry them all, and the weaker species of the human race will die out.[4] Second, Lons Von Liebenfeld followed Gobenal's writing with his own, called *Theological Zoology.* In it, Von Liebenfeld says that some races are superior to other races. Then he ranked them: most superior was the Germanic race or the Arians, followed by other significant races such as the Celts, the French, the Spanish, but then he claimed that climates influence the ability of races; so he ranked the Portuguese, the Slavs of Russia, and the Turks next, kind of far down the list. Closest to the bottom fell the Africans, then lastly he placed the Jews, the most inferior race of all.[4]

Hitler lived in Vienna at the time of these writings, and it was logical for him to believe the way he did when we view how Darwinism was applied to the human race through these two writers…and they were best sellers!

DARWINISM

One of the philosophers that heavily influenced Darwin was Thomas Malthus. He wrote a book in the early 19th century, *The Principles of Population*. Malthus was an Anglican preacher and said, "Poverty exists in the world to cause starvation to cause people to do hard work and therefore virtuous behavior."[4] In other words, poverty and starvation are God-given

> JUST FOR THE RECORD:
> The only improved life for humans is a life surrendered to the God of Abraham, Isaac and Jacob in His son, Jesus!

tools to make people better. Malthus said the population will eventually outrun resources and result in famine and starvation; but it is ultimately for the good because starvation will develop improved life forms. Malthus influenced Darwin with this idea of improved life forms.

In 1859, Darwin wrote *The Origin of Species*. When people read it, it troubled the moral order of society even though it had nothing to do with morals. Darwin's former mentor wrote in a personal letter to Darwin, long before the Holocaust, "Were it possible to break it (the moral order), humanity in my mind would suffer a damage that might brutalize it and sink the human race into a lower grade of degradation than any into which it has fallen since its written records tell us of its history."[1]

Darwinism undermined the moral value of life because evolutionary progress became the moral imperative. It is aided by the advance of eugenics (the concept of improving the human species through manipulating biology). Later those in Darwinism advocated the use of euthanasia and infanticide. Some argued that evolutionary progress in racial competition would cause a struggle for existence among the races. Hitler took these ideas, combined with his anti-Semitism to initiate the Holocaust.

HAECKEL

The German science fields really embraced Darwinism. The most famous German scientist who was a Darwinist was Earnest Haeckel. He suggested that even morality was developed by evolution. His two books were the most popular non fiction books in Germany. Haeckel touted in the *Wonders of Life* (1904) that humans with the worst character are throwbacks to earlier, more primitive stages of evolutionary development.[2] The vast majority of the people were promoting this evolutionary theory. Promoting eugenics led to more available abortion, euthanasia, and prevention of certain races from propagating, like the U.S. did with Native Americans and Africans in the 1920s. This sterilization and death was acceptable, because if one believes this Hegelian theory as applied to biology, sterilization logically leads to a higher form of the human race. Most of the people promoting these ideas were scientists and physicians. The few opposed were philosophers and sociologists. Science was driving this.

After Darwinism became popular, the sanctity of human life promoted by John Locke and the Declaration of Independence lost their emphasis. Abortion, infanticide, euthanasia and suicide became increasingly popular. German psychologists adopted the view of the human mind of Hackle. It all came out of the theory of evolution, and Hegel's worldview! By the late 19th and early 20th century, most German scientists recognized that there was biological inequality among the races. This inequality is fundamental to Darwinian Theory.

Most of this information is shocking, because it is totally rejected today. But why was it abandoned? It's not because of science or logic, but because of the Holocaust.[3] Because if people believe purely in Darwinian science and its offshoots, they will come to the logical conclusion that races are unequal. Some are superior to others. There is no question about it, *if* someone buys into Darwinism! Some groups will evolve more quickly than others. All the intellectuals in Europe and many in the U.S. believed it! It was the most advanced, politically correct thinking of the time!

The dominant view was that those with less value were the non-European races, the disabled or the economically unproductive. Among *some* of these leading thinkers, those people were considered worthless. In 1868, a list of 10 different species of humans ranked according to their value was circulated.[4] The influence of psychiatry grew in the late 19th and early 20th century, through Freud and others. Two leading German professors in 1920, Karl Binding and Alfred Hoche wrote in their book, *The Permission of Life to Destroy Life Unworthy of Life*, "There is a need to segregate the inferior so they cannot reproduce."[7] They warned people against a false compassion for the inferior since "our healthy offspring have the right to be protected from decay through those who are genetically"[7] less than.

Thomas Huxley wrote in his 1861 book, *Man's Place in Nature vol VII*, "Men differ more widely from one another than they do from the Apes; while the lowest Apes differ as much, in proportion, from the highest, as the latter does from Man."[6(section 107, para 3)] In plainer

English Huxley is saying, "The differences between the lowest humans and the highest apes are smaller than the differences between the lowest and highest humans." By the end of the 19th century, racial distinctions had moved from just noting the differences between European and non-European people to the supremacy of the German race to even other European races, while denigrating the Jews.

Robert Chambers in 1844, in *The Natural History of Creation* became an advocate for killing the weak and the sick. It is the logical consequence of Darwinism. The weak and sick are burdens to society and according to the logic of this theory, they should be eliminated. Darwinism makes the death of inferior people seem inevitable, even efficient. It became a moral good to kill the lower forms of life. The Darwinian key to progress is the annihilation of lower races.

THE HERERO REVOLT ANNIHILATED THE LOWER RACES OF NAMIBIA

Killing the weak was first practiced in Namibia in 1904 during a revolution in a German Colony. The Herero tribe rose up against the German colonial government. The German general who oversaw the colony was a Darwinist, and he wiped out 65,000 of the Hereros, 80% of their population, because he viewed the revolt as a racial war. Scholars today have tried to say that this "revolution of race" had nothing to do with the Nazis; however, one of the top Nazi leaders perpetrating the Holocaust was Hermann Göring. Göring's father was at one time the German colonial governor of Namibia. There is still a street named after him in Swakopmund. I see a bit more of a connection than today's scholars. Göring had been steeped in Darwinist thinking from childhood and it was an easy transition for him to kill Jews.

233

Darwin's later gruesome writing, *The Descent of Man*, says, "At some future period, civilized races of man will almost certainly exterminate and replace throughout the world the savage races."[5]

Haeckel used the destruction of the American Indians and the Australian Aborigines as an example of *good*. In his thinking it was the natural order of the races.

So take all this craziness of progressive thinking that was prevalent even in the newspapers and apply it to a young Adolf Hitler. To Hitler this race bias was not amoral; he genuinely believed the world would be a better place without the inferior members of society. The Darwinian struggle for racial existence became the sole arbiter of morality in German society. They believed that they highest good is accomplished when you cooperate with the evolutionary process.

The prevalent strategy for dealing with inferior races was two pronged: One was Eugenics, manipulating biology to create a higher form of humanity, and the other was to improve the Aryan race and its struggle by initiating warfare outside of Germany. Therefore, the foundational idea of the Third Reich was that they were conquering the world for the betterment of the world.

The Jews, according to Hitler, were amoral, greedy, deceitful and the greatest threat to humanity. He read many books on racial struggle and combined those ideas with strong anti-Semitism.[4] The Jews being defined by race at this time, helped him wipe them out, because it was no longer a religious categorization of human beings.

Before WWI, Germany had been the leader in education, science, arts, in chemical industry and pharmacy, transportation, invention of appliances, and the top inventors for years. It was their identity. They were the most advanced society in the world, and the Jews were very much a part of society, even contributing to it! The change occurred in WWI, a catastrophe for Europe. There were staggering losses of men and property. The Allies couldn't break through the Axis lines. Revolutions were exploding around the world, in Russia especially. The Kaiser and Italy's Monarchy collapsed; Austro-Hungary collapsed. Because of the defeat of the Ottoman Empire new nations were being founded all over Eastern Europe and the Middle East. WWI became the most world-changing war in history. Even today, all the conflict in the Middle East is leftover from WWI, because of the way the Allies carved up the new national boundary lines.

The German people were looking for an explanation. How could the most advanced society on the planet suffer such a humiliating defeat? The Treaty of Versailles made it even worse by imposing guilt on the Germans. The treaty declared that Germany was responsible for the war. The German Army was then stabbed in the back by civilian politicians who were Liberals, Communists, and Jews. The army leaders had questioned the advisability of going into the war, and they surmised that it was the Jews (again!) who had destroyed them and undermined morale.

Fear and uncertainty followed the war and bred anti-Semitism in the 1920's. It actually became popular to hate the Jews. The steep reparations and ceding of German land to other nations enforced by the treaty became the seeds for future conflict.

את

NEW GERMAN GOVERNMENT

From 1919-1933 Germany had a new government: A representative, constitutional government modeled after the United States. Germany instituted a parliament called the Reichstag. Most Germans opposed the new government because they identified it with the humiliation of the war. Then the combined cost of the war and reparation payments brought about a staggering financial crisis. In November 1921, the exchange rate between the German Mark and the U.S. dollar was 8:1. In 1922, it was 8,000,000:1.[4] That's 8 billion German marks to 1 U.S. dollar! The German currency was worthless. Savings and fixed incomes completely collapsed. The world powers tried to revalue and prop up the German mark, but it never recovered its previous value.

In south Bavaria, several new political parties arose, many were right-wingers, who attacked the new government. One in particular was called the National Socialist German Workers party, or Nazis. Until 1923 or 1924 it was just like the other parties, but then the Nazis attempted a coup of the new German government. They were led by Adolf Hitler. They were crushed by the German military and police. Hitler was tried publicly and became a national political celebrity. He was sentenced to five years in prison, and served one. There he wrote *Mein Kamf* (translated: My Story or My Struggle), outlining in chilling detail his plan to conquer the world and destroy world Jewry.

In October 1929, the Great Depression hit the world, including the United States. Germany had been propped up by loans from American banks. When the American banks called the loans, Germany completely collapsed. In 1932, German unemployment was 30%! There was no "welfare." People were starving and blaming the government for the problem. Hitler saw it as an opportunity. In September 1930, the Nazis had 12 elected representatives in the Reichstag. In 1932, they gained 107 seats.[4] They were the largest party now, and in one year, through political manipulation, Hitler became the logical representative for the Chancellor, or "president." Hitler just wanted a chance to govern for four years and to lead

Germany out of its depression and re-establish its prominence. Sounds pretty good; why not? He was offering hope and change!

In 1933, Hitler was appointed chancellor of Germany. Let me emphasize: this was not a coup, but a democratic election! The Nazis had a simple platform: Those responsible for the German defeat in WWI would be defeated and destroyed![4] The Jews would be removed from German life.

HITLER'S OBJECTIVES WERE SYSTEMATIC[4]:

1ST FROM 1933-1935 Hitler consolidated power internally. For the first 2.5 years he devoted himself to domestic issues, and consolidated political power. Labor unions were outlawed, opposing political parties were harassed and closed, concentration camps were established for dissidents, and public industry was shut down and taken over by the government. Student group leadership was taken over by government officials.[4]

2ND FROM 1933-1936 Germany was a Federalist country. Hitler destroyed the Weimar Constitution. In 1936, Hitler issued a decree appointing Himmler Chief of the German Police and head of the SS.

3RD IN 1935 AND 1936 Hitler turned to foreign affairs. He disavowed the disarmament from the Treaty of Versailles. He held a military draft and re-armed Germany. He started a series of work projects to put Germans back to work, such as the building of the Autobahn and the design and manufacture of the Volkswagen. Since Hitler was putting Germans back to work it looked like he was fulfilling his promises. There was no more depression. In March 1936, Hitler sent troops into the Rhineland in violation of the treaty and no one stopped him; he claimed it was still German territory.

By November 1937, Hitler knew his foreign enemies would not stand up to him. In March 1938, Hitler marched into Austria claiming the same thing as in the Rhineland. There was no fighting because Hitler sent people ahead to form a new government of German-speaking Austrians. No one reacted, and he just kept moving forward with his agenda.

Next was Czechoslovakia. He claimed that 600,000 people of Czechoslovakia were ethnically German and should be part of Germany. European powers agreed to Hitler taking on new boundaries. He expanded and expanded.

Hitler ran into a problem as he expanded though; he had to deal with more Jews.

THE JEWISH PROBLEMS

In October 1933, Hitler issued a series of decrees that banned Jews from certain occupations. No civil service or work in the universities, etc. It was very common throughout their history so the Jews were used to it. Then Hitler got the Reichstag to pass the Enabling Act in 1933 which gave all power to Hitler to rule by executive decree. (Because of the "state of emergency" in Germany, Hitler said he needed to take control to bring the country out of its problems.) After the Enabling Act, he had complete control of the country, and his laws became more numerous and brutal over time. In 1934 and 1935 there were 700,000 Jews in Germany, all successfully assimilated in the community. Hitler's goal was to make life unbearable for the Jews and destroy them. He created laws to escalate this destruction by first defining who the Jews were. In September 1935, he passed the Nuremburg Laws to "protect the German blood."

NUREMBURG LAWS:

1.) Prohibit intermarriage and sex between Germans and Jews.

2.) Define a half-Jew as anyone with one parent who is Jewish and a quarter-Jew as anyone with one grandparent who is a Jew. Anyone with at least one-quarter Jewish blood was to be set aside. The horror of this law was redeemed in Israel's Law of Return, in which anyone with at least one grandparent who is Jewish can make *Aliyah*, meaning they can return to the Land of Israel and become a citizen.

Hitler enacted more laws. The Jews were forbidden to shop in certain places or ride certain trains. Jews born after the 1935 Nuremburg Laws were not German citizens. Jews lost property and citizenship. In 1938 every Jew was required to adopt 'Sarah' or 'Israel' as a middle name. Hitler's goal was to identify the Jews. Then a red J was required on all Jewish documents. In September 1941, Jews were required to wear a yellow Jewish star with "Juden" written in the middle. The goal was to isolate, discriminate and destroy the Jewish people.

In March 1938, Germany overran Austria, and with Austria came more Jews. Three hundred thousand of them. The SS loosed a pogrom in Vienna where Jews were forced to scrub sidewalks and were beaten and killed. Thousands were sent to concentration camps. Jews continued to emigrate, but where could they go? Some sheltered in Czechoslovakia, Austria, Soviet Union, France, Romania, Poland, and some to China, some to Palestine. The U.S. received 90,000, and 38,000 made it to Latin America. The problem is most of those other countries were conquered by the Germans. So those Jews merely delayed death for a while.

In the spring of 1938, Eichmann, working under Himmler in the SS was given the responsibility of leading the Central Office for Jewish Immigration in Vienna. He wanted to Aryanize Vienna and the surrounding areas by removing Jews and confiscating Jewish property. By the fall of 1938, half the Jews had left Vienna. In October 1938, Germany attacked Czechoslovakia and suddenly had many more Jews to deal with. Now, other countries *finally* objected! And Chamberlain of England struck a deal to allow Hitler to keep Czechoslovakia as long as he would not expand the German borders any further.

THE SPARK THAT LAUNCHED THE HOLOCAUST: NOVEMBER 7, 1938

A young Jewish man named Hirschel Grenspan, a polish Jew, whose parents had been forced out of Germany, entered the German embassy in Paris and killed the Secretary to the Ambassador. Hitler responded, "See what the Jews are up to! They are out to get us!" On November 8, 1938, Himmler spoke to the German generals in Munich. "A new war is coming, unlike any war. It is the Germans against world Jewry. And one will win." With that began *Krystalnacht*, "The Night of the Breaking of Glass."

The night of November 9-10, 1938, Joseph Goebbles unleashed the *Krystalnacht* throughout Germany as a national violence against all Jews. Germans, both private citizens and military personnel, destroyed 1000's of synagogues and homes and shops. Property damage amounted to the 100's of millions of dollars.[4] The world was completely stunned! Roosevelt recalled the ambassador to Germany and cancelled all U.S. contracts with them. Hitler decided *Krystalnacht* was too inefficient and too public a way of dealing with the Jews; to him, it was irrational. Two months later, Hitler moved Eichman from Vienna back to Berlin to come up with a quieter plan to eliminate the Jews.

In Germany most of the Jewish population lived near each other; so if they all disappeared, Hitler knew people would notice and the world would respond. Hitler needed a distraction. So they came up with a deportation strategy and devised a "national emergency" to camouflage their movement: Germany invaded Poland in September 1939.

Within two weeks, Himmler and Heydrich killed as many Jewish leaders as they could. Their strategy was implemented like this: after the military invaded an area, the SS would send in motorized units that would shoot as many Jews as possible. Then the "occupational protocols"[4] were begun:

- concentrate the Jews in ghettos
- register all of them
- be sure that each ghetto city is located next to the railroad lines.

The Germans had only been dealing with a couple hundred thousands Jews at a time until this point, but in conquering Poland, the German Nazis acquired another 3.5 million Jews. In conquering Western Europe in early 1940, Hitler got another 1 million Jews and emigration from those countries became impossible.

On July 2, 1940, Herman Goring (the SS's #2 man) assigned Reinhard Heydrich the task of finding a "final solution for the Jewish question of Europe." They decided to kill them all, men, women, and children. Using bullets was too inefficient and expensive, so they began to use carbon monoxide gas.

"In early December, the first extermination camp, Chelmno, went into operation. This was not just a concentration camp, but a death camp! There Jews were murdered with carbon monoxide gas generated by large diesel engines that pumped gas into chambers."[8]

Concentration Camp System

In August 1940, the first Auschwitz camp in Poland was opened for political dissidents. It was formerly a brick armory with a large courtyard. They added a watch tower and barbed wire around the perimeter. Rudolf Hess was appointed commandant.

By 1941, plans were in the works for different levels of camps; one was a work camp; the well-known Dachau was one of these. Then there were death camps: Auschwitz II was one of these; it was also known as Birkenau because of its location near a forest called by that name. Birkenau was built under the guise as a camp for prisoners of war. Hess, the commandant of Auschwitz I, was ordered to build this camp and his orders were changed to expand from previous plans. He used Jewish labor from Auschwitz to build it.

Hitler's plans for Auschwitz II and III also contained a secret plan for taking over Russia. Its code name was Barbarossa. In December 1940, he and his generals decided to attack Russia the following June. Hitler's main enemy was the Jews, but his secondary enemy was the communists. He declared that communists were infected with Jews. (Stalin's inner circle contained Jews in key and advisory positions.)

Barbarossa

In June 1941, the attack on Russia began. It was three-pronged. The northern army section surrounded Leningrad and nearly starved the people to death. Then a second group reached the edge of Moscow and attacked for about a year. The southern route was eventually blocked at Stalingrad. As Hitler attacked, German forces rolled across Poland (held by Russia) and Belarus, (both with huge Jewish populations). As the military advanced the SS would follow with their mobile killing units. But German leadership called it ineffective because it used up so much ammunition.

One particular attack in Babi Yar, a little town just outside of Kiev, led to one of the most horrific Jewish slaughters. They rounded up all the Jews in the city and brought them out and shot them in pits. Here is a firsthand account from 1941.

THE TRUCK DRIVER'S ACCOUNT OF BABI YAR[9]

There was a notice placed in the city and surrounding, "Kikes of Kiev and surrounding cities, on Monday, September 29, you are to appear by 7 AM with your possessions, money, documents and valuables, and warm clothing at Melnikova Street, next to the Jewish cemetery. Failure to appear is punishable by death."

The following is an eye witness account from a truck driver that day:

One day I was instructed to drive my truck outside the town of Kiev; I was accompanied by a Ukrainian. It must have been about 10 o'clock. On the way there, we overtook Jews carrying luggage. Marching on foot in the same direction we were traveling. There were whole families. The farther we got out of town the denser the columns became. Piles of clothing lay in a large open field. The piles of clothing were my destination. The Ukrainian showed me how to get there. After we had stopped in the area, near the piles of clothes, the truck was immediately loaded up with clothing. This was carried out by Ukrainians. I watched what happened when the Jews, men, women and children arrived.

The Ukrainians led them by a number of different places where one after the other they had to remove their luggage and then their coats, shoes and over-garments and also underwear. They had to leave their valuables in a designated place. There was a special pile for each article of clothing. It all happened very quickly and anyone who hesitated was kicked or pushed by the Ukrainians to keep them moving. I don't think it was even a minute from the time each Jew took off his coat before he was standing there completely naked. No distinction was made between men, women, and children. One would have thought that the Jews who came later would have had a chance to turn back when they saw the others in front of them having to undress. It still surprises me today that this did not happen.

Once undressed, the Jews were led into a ravine that was about 150 meters long, 30 meters wide and 15 meters deep. Two or three narrow entrances led to this ravine, through which the Jews were channeled. When they reached the bottom of the ravine, they were seized by members of the Schutz-Polietzi (German police) and made to lie down on top of Jews who had already been shot. This all happened very quickly. The corpses were literally in layers. A police marksman came along and shot each Jew in the neck with a submachine gun at the spot where he was lying. When the Jews reached the ravine, they were so shocked by the horrifying scene that they completely lost their will. It may even have been that the Jews themselves lay down in rows to wait to be shot. There were only two marksmen carrying out the executions. One was working at one end of the ravine and one at the other at the other end. I saw these marksmen stand on the layers of corpses and shoot one after another. The moment one Jew had been killed the marksmen would walk across the bodies of the executed Jews to the next Jew who had meanwhile lain down, and shoot him. It went on this way uninterrupted with no distinction between men women and children. The children were kept with their mothers and shot with them. I only saw this scene briefly, but when I got to the bottom of the ravine, I was so shocked by the terrible sight, I could not bear to look for long. In the hollow, I saw that there were already three rows of bodies lined up over a distance of about 60 meters. How many layers of bodies there were on top of each other, I could not see. I was so astonished and dazed by the sight of the twitching and blood-smeared bodies that I could not properly register the details. In addition to the two marksmen, there was a packer at each entrance to the ravine. These packers were (police) whose job it was to lay the victims on top of the other corpses so that all the marksman had to do as he passed was fire a shot.

When the victims came along the path to the ravine and, at the last moment saw the terrible scene, they cried out in terror. The very next moment they were already being knocked over by the packers and made to lie down with the others. The next group of people could not see this terrible scene because it took place around a corner. Most people put up a fight when they had to undress and there was a lot of screaming and shouting. Ukrainians did not take any notice; they just drove them down as quickly as possible into the ravine entrances. From the undressing area you could not make out the ravine, it was windy and cold and the shots could not be heard in the undressing area. This is why I think that the Jews did not understand in time what lay ahead of them. I still wonder today why the Jews did not try to do something about it. Masses kept on coming from the city to this place...still under the impression they were being resettled."

Jews numbering 33,000 perished in two days in that ravine!

Increased Efficiency

From June 1941 to August 1942, these mobile units killed about 500,000 Jews from the Baltic Sea to the Black Sea. But it was too messy, too inefficient and took too much material. So Hitler built six extermination camps throughout Poland. These camps are where the vast majority of Jews were killed in the war.

By fall 1942, the German scientists re-discovered a pesticide that had been outlawed because it was too dangerous, called Zyklon. They tweaked it a bit and called it Zyklon B, and they put it in canisters. Once exposed to air this chemical compound releases hydrogen cyanide which is deadly to an entire room of people within about 20 minutes.

Initially the Jews who were murdered were buried, but it began to create sanitary problems, so the camps began to burn them. But the volume was overwhelming. Five railroad transports, bringing 5,000-7,000 people every DAY, five days a week. The two gas chambers in Auschwitz II could handle 1,500-2,000 people at once.

As the war intensity increased, the number of camp workers also increased. By 1942 there were hundreds of thousands of non-German workers working in the camps, Ukrainians and Latvians, Estonians, and others. Jews were required to do all the work involved in the killing of Jews in the camps, enforced by these workers with guns.

The train would come in, and "ramp duty" Jews who spoke several languages would greet the Jews like this: "Don't worry, you're being resettled here for your own protection. Many of you will be showered down from your long trip and then you'll be settled into comfortable surroundings." If anyone said anything about what was really happening, they'd be shot on the spot. So they lied.

Jews would come off the trains to tables with SS members who decided where the Jews would go. Women, older men and children were directed straight into the gas chamber "showers." Stronger men would be relocated to one of the labor camps and some of the young, pretty women would be given to the soldiers as prostitutes.

Those slated for death would be sent in and greeted by a second group of Jews known as the "undressers" They would make sure that the Jews put all their clothes and valuables into compartments in an area that looked like a dressing room. Then they directed them into the gas chamber itself. As soon as the doors closed, the undressers took the clothing and possessions, and loaded them into trucks where they were shipped back to Germany. The Jews were told to congregate around the shower heads, but they weren't shower heads. The pipes actually led to an outside opening, and the SS would take two canisters of the Zyklon B and drop them into the pipes.

Then a third group of Jews, "body removers," would enter through the back door and untangle the bodies that had formed pyramids where they climbed on top of each other, fighting for the last breathable air. They had to search for any hidden valuables and remove gold teeth and cart the bodies to the ovens.

The fourth group of Jews were the "oven-worker Jews." Every day they would take the bodies of their brothers and place them in the ovens and burn them. Some of these workers *did* survive and were an absolute emotional and spiritual mess when freed.

THE SOVIET UNION FINALLY RESPONDED

We assume that WWII was won by Eisenhower, the West and D-day, but the truth is that if Russia had not stepped up and kept the Nazi forces divided, the Allies would have been overrun. In winter 1942-43, Russia was able to stop Hitler in Stalingrad and Moscow, slowly pushing them back. The Russian front came within a whisper of falling. If Russia had fallen, Germany would have been unstoppable. The Nazis were finally defeated on the eastern front in spring of 1944.

The Nazi generals saw the end coming with their eastern defeat and requested that Hitler reallocate the work camp and death camp resources to the war effort, but he refused and increased the death pace. More Jews were murdered in 1944 and 1945 than in all the time before. Hitler's goal was to obliterate them. In his mind it was for the betterment of the whole world.

The Allies had learned about the death camps by 1942, but did nothing. In 1944, Churchill requested that Eisenhower at least bomb the railroad lines to slow down the efficiency of the killing, but Eisenhower refused to separate his military might from the primary mission to destroy the German military.

By 1945, Berlin was surrounded by the Russians and the Allied forces. Soon thereafter, Berlin fell, Hitler committed suicide and the war was over. Then the camps were opened for the first time. When the photos hit the press in the West, it shocked the world. The West had not known that this level of evil existed.

Twenty-seven million people in the Soviet Union were killed in the war. Seven million were military. Twenty *million* were civilians. Every family lost someone.

Six million Jews were put to death and 1.5 million of those were children.

Some of the countries that did a relatively good job of protecting the Jews were Norway, Denmark, the Netherlands, Italy and Hungary. Also there were Righteous Gentiles found in every country. People like Corrie ten Boom's family and the Schindlers.

The world was in shock, wondering how such an event could occur in the most educated society in the world. The Holocaust changed everything! It changed the way the world looked at life. The idea that man is essentially good, was completely altered after the Holocaust. It changed the orientation of the Church toward the Jewish people. It took an event of this magnitude to cause reconsideration of Christian theology after 2,000 years. Most leaders recognized that even though the Holocaust was not a Christian event, Christian anti-Semitism for so many centuries laid the foundation for this kind of hatred. *But* the good news is that it caused the Church to repent! The Catholic Church was first in 1962-63. They rejected the idea of replacement theology (on the surface) and that Jews were responsible for the death of Jesus. Other denominations followed their lead.

One part of modern society that has not yet recognized their culpability in the holocaust is the scientific world, where the Darwinism that made the Holocaust possible is still rampant. When there is no repentance, people continue down the same road toward destruction. Today, Darwinists have rejected the Eugenics movement, and the idea that some races are superior to others on a scientific basis, but not on a moral basis. They do not recognize that this is what led to the Holocaust. That Darwinistic thinking led to the Holocaust is hidden; this path is not traced out plainly in many history books. If repentance does not come, the door remains open for the Holocaust to happen again.

End Notes

1. Personal correspondence between Adam Sedgewick and Charles Darwin November 24, 1859 retrieved March 14, 2014 from http://www.creationstudies.org/Education/quotes.html

2. Haeckel, Ernt. 1904. Wonders of Life. Retrieved March 14, 2014 from http://www.egs.edu/library/ernst-haeckel/quotes/

3. Cowen, Jamie rabbi. 2011. Jewish History Course. RIHOP, Richmond, VA Spring 2011.

4. As quoted by Rabbi Jamie Cowen. 2011. Jewish History Course. RIHOP, Richmond, VA Spring 2011.

5. Darwin, C. 1871. *Descent of Man.*

6. Huxley. 1861. *Man's Place in Nature. Vol VII* Selected essays. Of man's relation to the lower animals. section 107 para 3 retrieved March 15, 2014 from http://aleph0.clarku.edu/huxley/CE7/RelM-L-A.html

7. Binding, K. and Hoche, A. 1920. *The Permission to Destroy Life Unworthy of Life*

8. Yad Vashem. (n.d.). The Holocaust. FAQ. *What were the extermination camps? When did they start to function? And what was their purpose?* Retrieved April 27, 2010 from http://www1.yadvashem.org/yv/en/holocaust/resource_center/faq.asp

9. The Babi Yar truck driver's account was read in Jamie Cowan's Jewish History Seminar and transcribed from that recording. Here is another on line resource of the same recollection: Retrieved March 18, 2014 from http://www.executedtoday.com/2010/09/29/1941-babi-yar-massacre-holocaust/

12

WHY ARE NAMES SO IMPORTANT TO GOD?

It may be fairly obvious now that we have studied a bit of Hebrew, the importance God places on the function of a person's name or what something is called, versus the Greek way of thinking in appearance and abstract. God can speak so much through names. Remember the genealogy prophecy we studied in Genesis 5? All those names spoke to the individual's destiny and purpose, and when placing the 10 generation's name meanings back to back it created a prophetic message for the coming of a Savior that God was speaking from the very beginning.

Several times in scripture God changed a person's name. Other stories tell of how man changed a person's name. Later in history, with the translation of the Bible, men again changed names (specifically in the King James Bible upon which most of the others are based).

It might be helpful here to point out the difference between the words *transliterate* and *translate*. To transliterate is to take the phonetic sounds of another language and spell the word in such a way as to facilitate repetition of the same sound as the original in the new language. To translate is to take the original meaning of the foreign word and substitute a "known" word with the same meaning. Translated words rarely sound alike, and it can take more or fewer words to translate concepts between languages. Word-for-word translations rarely make sense in a new language so translators shuffle words around to bring ease of reading in the new language. Transliteration is most common among names of people and places. Sometimes a translator who has transliterated a name will then substitute a common name in his culture for a foreign name that sounds (somewhat) similar to the transliterated name. Craig Bluemel[12] says it like this:

> During the 15th through 18th centuries A.D., when the Bible was being translated and circulated to use into the English language, certain alphabetic letters that were common to English, such as the letters 'J' and 'V' were considered phonetically incompatible with the phonetic sound of the Hebrew 'Y' (in its transliterated form) and in many places, the 'W.'

Consider our Bible's translator's changing of Yisrael to Israel, Yahweh to Jehovah, and Yudah to Judah.

But what is the outcome of a changed name? Whether it is God-directed or man- or translator-directed, what changes? How does the change influence someone's function and destiny? Can it change

252

anything after they are dead? Let's start back with Abram and check
it out.

ABRAM TO ABRAHAM AND SARI TO SARAH

To discuss Abraham and Sarah, we first need to discuss God's name.
Remember from chapter 2 when we discussed the tetragrammaton,
God's name which we translate Yahweh or Jehovah? It is spelled:
yod, hey,vav, hey. יהוה

The Hebrew letter hey ה means spirit[1] and it is found twice in
God's unspeakably holy name.

For Abraham and Sarah, when He changed their names, Yahweh
(yod, hey, vav, hey) donated to each of them, one letter hey from His
name.

Abram + ה = Abrהam or Abraham
Sari + ה = Sarה or Sarah

God inserted Himself into their destinies and functions. In donating a
hey ה to both Abram and Sari, He donated part of His spirit to each
of them[1] and therefore changed them to be more like Himself when
they mothered and fathered this new breed of people who would be
called by God's name. *Selah.*

How then does it change the meaning of their names and therefore
their function in life? Abram means exalted father, but Abraham
means father of many nations. That is quite an addition to this man's
destiny by bringing in the spirit (the ה hey) of the Living God.

Sari means "my princess" from the root word "sar" which means
prince. Sarah is closely related meaning "a princess." The Jewish

253

Encyclopedia (1906) explains the new meaning of a princess "because she was recognized generally as such"[2] based on her great beauty.

Reb Benzi puts it like this: Sari goes from "her role from simply (as) Abraham's wife, his little princess, to being G-d's princess, mother of nations, mother of kings, while remaining faithful and submissive to her husband as G-d commanded."[3]

We may think it is just semantics, but for Sarah, I'm sure it was quite a new role, especially nine decades into her life as Sari.

JACOB TO ISRAEL

In our Bible we read the name Jacob. But his given name was actually "Ya'acov." So this man had his name changed twice: once by God from Ya'acov to Yisrael, and then by a translator from Ya'acov to Jacob then to Israel. We discussed the meaning of "Israel" in chapter 2, but it bears repeating here.

Ya'acov literally means "supplanter." A supplanter is "one who wrongfully or illegally seizes and holds the place of another."[8] It comes from the Hebrew word *Vayeakveiki*. This long Hebrew word comes from the root word *Eikev* which means "heel." Ya'acov shares the same root word *Eikev*. Try sounding it out, the similarity is audible between *Eikev* and *Ya'acov*. Thus the connection is established between Ya'acov and supplanter.[9]

Ya'acov was grasping the heel of his twin Esau at birth, so he received a name which was related to the word heel. Perhaps it was a prophetic event even at the moment of the twins' birth of how Ya'acov would later trick his twin out of his firstborn birthright (Genesis 25:29-34) and Yitsak's (Isaac) father's blessing (Genesis 27). This man was certainly a trickster on his own (with some help from mom) against the world. His brother Esau even comments on Ya'acov's name:

> **Genesis 27:36** (NIV) Esau said, "Isn't he rightly named Jacob? This is the second time he has taken advantage of me: He took my birthright, and now he's taken my blessing!" Then he asked, "Haven't you reserved any blessing for me?"

The footnote in the NIV Bible says, "*Jacob* means *he grasps the heel*, a Hebrew idiom for *he takes advantage of* or *he deceives*."[10]

But then God got hold Ya'acov the Trickster at the end of himself out in the desert (Genesis 32). His large family was depending on him; he had abandoned or escaped his father-in-law, and was headed toward his angry twin who might kill him for returning. The Angel of the Lord wrestled with Ya'acov all night and at dawn renamed him Israel.

In most definitions you will see Israel defined as "struggles/wrestles with God" and while that certainly describes Ya'acov's night and life, there is more to it than that. Israel is a combination of two Hebrew words: "Isr" and "el." "El" means God and "isr" is from the root word "sar" meaning prince. So Israel means "Prince with God" Ya'acov's (Jacob's) destiny went from being a tricky cheater to being a prince *with* God. Wow, another major destiny change.

HOSHEA TO JOSHUA [11]
Numbers 13:4-15 describes the names of all the men who were chosen to spy out the land, one from each tribe. Hoshea, the son of Nun is listed as the representative for the tribe of Ephraim. Immediately following the list in verse 16 is the following statement: "These *are* the names of the men whom Moses sent to spy out the land. And Moses called Hoshea the son of Nun, Joshua."

So this name change was given by Moses. No reason is given, but it is interesting none-the-less because of a connection with a man of a name derived from this one many centuries down the road in the story of God.

In the original Hebrew this man's name was Oshea. יְהוֹשֻׁ (spelled: ayin, shen, vav, hey). Don't get confused with Oshea, Hoshea or Hosea, Yehoshua, or Joshua, we are talking about the same man: the man who led Israel into the Promised Land after Moses died.

Oshea is found as a verb in other places in scripture, usually meaning "to deliver someone from the danger of defeat." Oshea means deliverer or "He will save." Its root word is *Yasha* meaning "to help, deliver or save, to free or comfort."

When Moses changed "Oshea" to "Yehoshua" (In English we use Joshua instead of Yehoshua), the prefix Moses added "Yeh" is the beginning of the name *Yahweh*. Now that Oshea's name is Yehoshua, his name means "Yahweh delivers" or "Yahweh will save (from defeat)" or "Yahweh will free or bring comfort." What a difference in function the "Yeh" makes. Now God is the one who is doing all the work and Yehoshea's life sings a different tune.

Our English version of Yehoshua is "Joshua." It goes back to the lack of a J sound in Hebrew; it was added to the transliterated version of Oshea to sound more familiar to the new language speakers.

Craig Bluemel[12] says that Jews continued to use the name Yehoshea after the Babylonian Exile but condensed it to Yeshua. Does that sound familiar? So our name "Joshua" was actually the same name as Yeshua—the name from which our name "Jesus" was derived. Isn't it interesting to see that in different generations these two men with the same name provide the same function for their people? Joshua offered the truth of a situation in the Promised Land even though the people did not believe his report. Forty years later Joshua led the next generation in a campaign to make that land their own. He saved his people from living in the physical desert forever. Jesus/Yeshua also offered the truth to His people on the situation of the Promised Land of their hearts. Some rejected His assessment of their sin, some accepted His assessment and received life for death. Jesus/Yeshua saved His people *and* became life to the Gentiles, keeping people from having to live in a spiritual desert forever.

Interestingly, one other man is called by this same name, Hoshea, in scripture, though you might not recognize it because the "sh" sound of the Hebrew letter shen was changed to an "s" sound in this transliteration: Hosea. What was Hosea's function? He was a prophetic representation of God when Hosea married a prostitute who kept running away to other men. Hosea chased after her, saving her (even from her own foolish choices), bringing her home and accepting her back again and again, just like God does for Israel. It is a prophetic picture of what Joshua did and what Jesus did. All three men had their destiny and function spelled out in their name.

DANIEL TO BELSHAZZAR; HANANIAH, MISHAEL, & AZARIAH TO SHADRACH, MESHAC & ABED NEGO [4]

These four young men had their names changed, not by God but by a Babylonian king's eunuch. And it was not a blessing for them, except that being called by a "false name" must have been a constant reminder of their true identity. These name changes were a direct attack of the enemy on their identity: All of these Hebrews' new names were names of Babylonian gods.

DANIEL means "God is my judge" or "God rules me" based on the Hebrew verb *din* meaning "to judge, to contend or to plead," which connects more in the realm of governing than the judicial judgment we tend to think of. When breaking *Daniel* down, Dan means judge;

the Yod (i-sound in Dan-I-el) denotes possession, the "my" part of the definition; and adding the "el" to the end designates God (from the abbreviated form of *Elohim*). Dan is also one of the twelve tribes of Israel.

Daniel was of royal lineage (Daniel 1:3) and carried the function and character of Elohim in his name before the chief of the Babylonian king's eunuch changed it to Belteshazzar (Daniel 1:3-7). Most sources say this new name means "Bel, protect the life of the king." I wonder if over time the name *Bel* had slid away from the name Ba'al. It makes sense because Bel has no particular reference in the god-list, yet the name Beltshazzar asks for protection for the life of a king, and only a "god" could do that.

Things take on an even more interesting twist with the boys from the fiery furnace.

HANANIAH in Hebrew means "Jehovah is gracious." Hananiah's name was changed to Shadrach which means "command of Aku (moon god)." So Hannaniah's name meaning went from "grace" to "command" and Jehovah, the all powerful, never changing, to some false moon god that changes constantly. What an attack on Hannaniah's very way of thinking.

MISHAEL in Hebrew means "who belongs to God." It is related to the Hebrew name Michael, meaning "Who is like God?" though not the same name. Mishael's name was changed to "who is like Aku (moon god)?" This name change was direct affront to Mishael's destiny and function of becoming like Jehovah and to Whom Mishael belonged.

AZARIAH in Hebrew means "Jehovah helps." His name was changed to Abednego. Abed means "servant" and Nego was the Babylonian god of wisdom. Again the new name was the direct opposite of

258

Azariah's real name and destiny. Instead of being helped by the all-knowing God Jehovah, his false name implied that Azariah should function as a servant of a false god of wisdom. Wow, what a difference.

את

NEW TESTAMENT NAME CHANGES

When jumping into the New Testament, most of the name changes were done years after the actual lives of the men who were renamed. My first thoughts of God changing names in the New Testament were Saul to Paul and Simon to Peter. We will take a closer look at both of those and get some truth according to the Scriptures.

When the Greek Bible of the New Testament changed the people's names to Greek names, it diminished the Jewishness of the Bible. Was it done on purpose? Yes. Was it done to sever any ties to the Jews? It is hard to know the motivations of men's hearts.[13] We know there were major issues, all rooted in pride, between the Jewish and Gentile Christians almost from the beginning, and it came from both sides, more from the lay people than the leaders in the beginning, but as decades passed and wounds increased, the leaders of the Jewish believers and the leaders of the Gentile believers were just as harsh to one another as the lay people had been. Whatever the motivation of the scribes and translators, the outcome of changing the people's names diminished the Jewishness of the Bible, both Old and New Testaments, in the minds of Gentiles. But for Jews, these changes separated the future Jews (any born after the changes were made) from seeing their Savior as described in the New Testament writings...writings *by* their Jewish ancestors. The New Testament was written by Jewish men, who followed a Jewish Messiah. Name changing opened the doorway in the coming millennia for the persecution of the Jews as "Christ killers," because it separated the Jews from their identity both in the minds of the Jews and Gentiles.

The name changes could reflect a scribe's or translator's desire to connect his own people to the Gentile-counterpart or the etymology of the Hebrew names so they didn't sound so foreign, to give his people something to hold onto, to create a grid of familiarity. That sounds nice. However digging beneath the surface, this help shows a man who doesn't trust God to supply the connections people need to the truth. He is trying to take the place of God by providing false connections that God didn't intend. While these name changes provided a Gentile with a familiar sound in his ear, the negative side is that the Gentile lost his Jewish roots of Christianity for 2,000 years.

The Jew suffered a much more lasting consequence. He was separated from Yeshua, because Shi'mon's testimony of the Meshach was published as "Peter's testimony of Christ," and Rabbi Shaul's understanding of the Ruach haKodesh was circulated as "the Holy Spirit is the third person of the trinity." (Yes, this is oversimplified, because throughout the ages there have always been men and women who are both Jewish and believe that Yeshua/Jesus is the Messiah). These name changes to make Gentiles more comfortable were too costly. It cost the eternal souls of Jews who saw Christianity as a cult that broke off from Judaism and went totally idolatrous, so the Jews would have nothing to so with it, even to study "the idolatry" for themselves. Once the names were changed, the Jews couldn't recognize their own Redeemer and people.

SIMON TO PETER
Simon to Peter is actually Shim'on to Simon to Cephas to Peter...Identity crisis in the making

Simon is actually the anglicized version of the Hebrew name
Shi'mon, which is what this disciple would have been called by his
friends and family.

Let's jump back to the well known story at Caesarea Philippi, when
Peter "got his name changed." Yeshua asks, "But who do *you* say that
I am?" Shim'on replies, "You are the Christ (really, he would have
called Him "Meshach"), the Son of the Living God." Yeshua replies,
"Blessed are you Shim'on bar Jonah, because my Father in heaven
revealed this to you. You didn't learn this from any human being.
From now on you will be called Peter, and on this rock I'll build my
church" (Matthew 16:16-18).

As only God can do, there are multiple things going on at once here.
First, Yeshua is not *renaming* Shim'on as Peter. He is giving him a
nickname. This is the only time Yeshua refers to him as Peter. Peter
means rock, and it is partly a play on words setting up Yeshua's next
statement. Not that on *Peter* Yeshua would build His church, but that
upon Shim'on Peter's statement of *revelation* He would build His
church. The revelation that Yeshua was Messiah is the foundation for
the update to the Covenant which would now become open for the
Gentiles. And "Peter" was a nickname like "Bear" or "Tiny" or "the
Rock."

In addition to all of that, there is an actual word in Hebrew *peter*.[5]
This Hebrew word is what the Hebrew speakers would have heard in
this circumstance. *Peter* in Hebrew means "first to open the womb."
Whoa! Yeshua is telling Shi'mon Peter that he is the very first man on
earth to recognize and accept Him as savior. Doesn't that bring a
whole other level of understanding to this story? This *peter* statement
does not diminish in any way that Mary and Joseph, the shepherds or
Elizabeth and Zechariah believed Jesus was the Messiah, but they all
heard it from angels, not by revelation. Shi'mon Peter was the

firstborn among men to understand/walk by revelation that Jesus was the Messiah and put his declaration out there into words, as almost every man after him would walk by revelation and declaration.

Rabbi Sha'ul to Apostle Paul

Sha'ul (anglicized to Saul) was *also* called Paul, he did not change his name. It comes from Acts 13:9 which says, "Then Saul, who also *is called* Paul, filled with the Holy Spirit, looked intently at him".

Paul was Sha'ul's Roman name, the same way people today have given names and Hebrew names. This was not an uncommon Jewish custom through the ages in order to adapt to their surroundings as strangers in strange lands. They could receive a Hebrew name and a cultural name at birth, or even to receive one and then *choose* the other later in life.

This particular name change was detrimental because it aided in the separation of the Jews and Gentiles, whom God intended to be one new man. The Gentiles, instead of integrating into Judaism, started "their own thing" based on Paul's teachings. But if the Gentiles had continued to call them Rabbi Sha'ul's teachings two things would have happened. First, they would have never grown to hate the Jews as ferociously as they did because the "they" of the Jews would still be the "us" of the combined New Covenant. No one is cruel to himself. Second, the Jews would not have so easily rejected the newer teachings/revelations of one of their own fellow Jewish rabbis, especially in later generations when they could study the scriptures and writings themselves.

You can try it yourself: Next time you are reading one of "Paul's" letters to the Churches, substitute "Rabbi Sha'ul" for "Apostle Paul" and "Synagogue" for "Church," because at the time Paul wrote, what we think of as the "Gentile Church" is still Gentiles meeting congruently with the Jews in their local synagogues or homes. This is what God intended from the beginning. Does this change alter your view of what you are reading? Truth usually does change things.

Here are some more names that might change the way you read your Bible:

- Ya'acov became Jacob or James
- Yosef became Joseph
- Miriam became Mary. All the Marys in the Bible were actually named Miriam, even Yeshua's mother.
- Elishaba/Elishava to Elizabeth
- Ezekiel, even though to our ear sounds Hebrew, it is actually Yechezqel (phonetically: Y-hes-kul).
- Yohannan to John or Jonathan

WHAT IS IN A NAME?

God has a purpose in your name. Do you know what He says about you in your name? Words and names talk about a person's function. Even the most worldly sounding name can hold a clue to your function in God's kingdom and in the earth.

In a small group some years ago I was talking with a friend of mine Brandi about name meanings. She didn't particularly like her name or its meaning, but God stopped our proceedings to download to her her function in life: Brandi, meaning "brandy" is a strong drink, just as she is strong. It is concentrated, with no excess water, just as Brandi is to function with no excess, watered-down teachings in her life. Brandy is sweet and has a delightful aftertaste, just as she is sweet and leaves a delightful aftertaste in the hearts of her friends after she has left them. Brandy is an after-dinner dessert liquor that calms, just as Brandi is a woman who calms people with her presence, especially after a heavy meal (i.e. a hard teaching or situation that is difficult to understand). It is made from fruit which is what Brandi is always to be walking in, the fruit of the Spirit: Love, joy, peace, patience, kindness, goodness, faithfulness, gentleness, and self-control (Galatians 5:22). Brandi will never look at her name again with the same disappointment, because God revealed her function in life through her name that day.

Ask the Lord about what your name means and about how you are to function in the earth according to your name's meaning. He loves to answer his children's questions, so have a pen and paper ready to record His reply.

END NOTES

1. Harnett, Paul. "What's in a Name?" Retrieved August 29, 2013 from http://www.jesus-resurrection.info/whats-in-name.html

2. The Jewish Encyclopedia. 1906. *Sarah(Sarai)* (Ber. 13a; Gen. R. xlvii. 1). Retrieved August 29, 2013 from http://www.jewishencyclopedia.com/articles/13194-sarah-sarai

3. Benzi, Haderekh Reb. April 17, 2009. Retrieved August 29, 2013 from http://kehilath-haderekh-benzi.blogspot.com/2009/04/why-did-g-d-change-sarais-name-to-sarah.html#!/2009/04/why-did-g-d-change-sarais-name-to-sarah.html
4. retrieved August 29, 2013 from http://dedication.www3.50megs.com/dan/belteshazzar.html

5. Thoene, Brodie & Brock. 2004. *Third Watch*. Tyndale House Publishing, Wheaton, Ill. p.331.

6. Notes on "Israel" meaning retrieved April 28, 2013 from http://www.ancient-hebrew.org/1_faqs_vocabulary.html#israel1.

7. Williams, James F. 2012. Probe Ministries International. Iakoboy (Greek) from Ya'acov (Hebrew) to Jacob to James retrieved September 30, 2013 from http://www.probe.org/site/c.fdKEIMNsEoG/b.4219723/k.9139/Why_Did_the_Book_of_Jacob_Get_Changed_to_the_Book_of_James.htm

8. Supplanter meaning. Retrieved September 30, 2013 from http://www.audioenglish.org/dictionary/supplanter.htm

9. Etymology of Ya'acov retrieved October 4, 2013 from http://wiki.answers.com/Q/The_word_supplant_means_to_replace_can_that_mean_in_a_bad_way_or_a_good_way_or_even_both

10. Holy Bible, New International Version®, NIV® Copyright © 1973, 1978, 1984, 2011 by Biblica, Inc.® Used by permission. All rights reserved worldwide. Retrieved October 4, 2013 from http://www.biblegateway.com/passage/?search=gen%2027:36&version=NIV

11. Uittenbogaard, Arie. 2000-2013. Abarim Publications. Retrieved October 4, 2013 from http://www.abarim-publications.com/Meaning/Bible_Names.html

12. Bluemel, Craig. (n.d.) Bible Answer Stand. Retrieved October 6, 2013 from http://bibleanswerstand.org/QA_savior.htm

13. If you are interested in more in depth research on the way language changes occur, try http://ebionite.org/names1.htm HOWEVER, they do not recognize Jesus as the Messiah and are not Christian, so I endorse only this name changing information on transliteration, not the whole website!

CONCLUSION

Christians should study Israel because Israel is a prototype of how God relates to mankind on a national level. He is great in mercy, abounding in love, always forgiving and pouring out grace. We should also study Israel, because it is the first half of our story and everything Christ and the cross are built on. Originally, Christ and the cross were called the "Messiah and redemption."

God is moving in our generation by revealing what He hid in Israel from ages past, in the Feasts of the Lord, and in Israel's history, and His faithfulness to them. He is uncovering more of His ultimate plan which has been hidden for generations, and we get to help Him by telling people of God's faithfulness to His chosen people. It didn't start 2,000 years ago; it started on the very first day! "From the rising of the sun to its going down The Lord's name *is* to be praised" (Psalm 113:3). Think of this rising sun even bigger than day to day, as in the original sunrise to the final sunset. It has been nearly 6,000 years of daily faithfulness!

God's faithfulness is important not only because it is His character and function, but also because there is coming a series of days when it will be difficult to trust that God is faithful and will fulfill every Word He has spoken. The last days are going to be horrific. God is going to make judgments against the earth and people that we will not understand. But if we have already seen Him be faithful to His Word to Israel in every intricate detail, it will be much easier for us to see Him as "in control" of the mess of our world in those days.

The Bible says that in the last days many will fall away from Him (Matthew 24:10-14). I do not want you or me to be in that group who falls away. If we decide now that we will follow God no matter what, that will help our hearts not become offended with God's actions in the future. Our hard decision is this: to trust Him in all His (strange and incomprehensible) decisions and ways!

The more we study His faithful history, His absolute detailed love for us, and His dynamic ultimate plan to provide for His Son a brilliant Bride dressed in white robes of righteousness, the easier it will be to trust His ways. And the easier it will be to provide understanding to those who come asking in the midst of the coming storm-to-end-all-storms!

PERSONAL NOTE FROM THE AUTHOR:

Dear Reader,

I began writing this conclusion while stranded in an ice storm 70 miles from home for 53 hours. (Ice is a big deal in Alabama). I found that it didn't matter how much "stuff" people had, like coats, shoes or food that helped them survive. It was the condition of their hearts. What I noticed, and got to participate in, was that a good attitude is just as contagious as a bad one. People stumbling in the door with a complaining, ungrateful attitude or blaming the weathermen, the mayor, or the road crews for not telling them about the ice, could easily be changed. I started reminding people that they were safe now, inviting them to sit down and relax on sofas or the floor, offering hot coffee—none of which belonged to me, but was set out for us by the business owners providing us shelter at their own expense. I got to remind people of what was really important, and Who was taking care of us and really providing for us, and I was privileged to see every single bad attitude change to a pleasant one. Not a single person denied that God was involved in getting him or her indoors and out of the harsh conditions.

The same will happen in those last days. We Christians need to be so attuned to God, and so unoffended by His actions that when difficulties come up that we cannot explain or understand, we point people to God, reminding them of His faithfulness. He will provide. He provided for the Israelites in the desert for 40 years, supplying food every day and shoes and clothes that didn't wear out. The Israelites' 40 years of a faithful God supplying their needs in the desert is not only an historical event, but a sign of how God will provide for those who belong to Him in the last days. God gave us a written record of His faithfulness so we would have a guide to follow and a great big God to believe in!

Shalom! And thanks for reading,

Kim Frolander

PS Please visit the website for art, books, and up-to-date information on joining a pilgrimage to Israel soon. Also, if you have a group of at least 10 friends to go with you, tours can be customized to suit your needs.

www.IsraelBasics.com

ALSO AVAILABLE FROM THIS AUTHOR

Paperback or Kindle version of the original *Israel Basics.: What Every Christian Should Know*. This 240+ page book covers the history, prophecy, some culture and language basics of the Chosen People. A great foundation for anyone, and it can be used as a small group study guide.

For anyone looking for a deeper look at the history of Ancient Israel who appears to have been lost from the Western historical record. God has an unfolding plan, prophesied in the blessings of Jacob and Moses at their deaths in Genesis 49 & Deuteronomy 33 for finding the "Lost Tribes" in the Last Days.

Visit the website for new offerings:

www.IsraelBasics.com

Made in the USA
San Bernardino, CA
26 April 2016